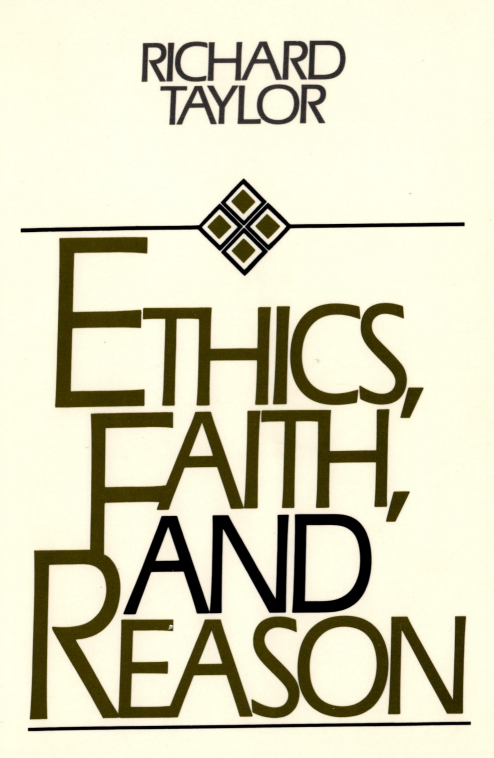

Richard Taylor

Ethics, Faith, and Reason

ETHICS,
FAITH,
AND REASON

ETHICS, FAITH, AND REASON

RICHARD TAYLOR

Leavitt-Spencer Professor of Philosophy
Union College

Prentice-Hall, Inc., Englewood Cliffs, New Jersey 07632

Library of Congress Cataloging in Publication Data

Taylor, Richard, 1919-
  Ethics, faith, and reason.

  Includes index.
  1. Ethics—Addresses, essays, lectures. I. Title.
BJ1012.T367 1985   171'.3   84-4844
ISBN 0-13-290552-3

Cover design: Ben Santora
Manufacturing buyer: Harry P. Baisley

Printed in the United States of America

10 9 8 7 6 5 4 3 2 1

ISBN 0-13-290552-3   01

Prentice-Hall International, Inc., *London*
Prentice-Hall of Australia Pty. Limited, *Sydney*
Editora Prentice-Hall do Brasil, Ltda., *Rio de Janeiro*
Prentice-Hall Canada Inc., *Toronto*
Prentice-Hall of India Private Limited, *New Delhi*
Prentice-Hall of Japan, Inc., *Tokyo*
Prentice-Hall of Southeast Asia Pte. Ltd., *Singapore*
Whitehall Books Limited, *Wellington, New Zealand*

To Joseph Fletcher——
theologian, scholar and friend

There must first be a disposition to excellence,
to love what is fine and loathe what is base.

Aristotle

Contents

Chapter 7

The Idea of Natural Law

Chapter 8

Cynics and Stoics

Chapter 9

Platonism and Ethical Relativism

Chapter 10

Aristotle's Ethics

PART THREE   DUTY *vs.* ASPIRATION

Preface

This book is a reorientation of ethics, almost a complete reversal of it. It repudiates the debilitating egalitarianism of modern ethics in favor of the ideals of the ancient pagan moralists. We have for so long been taught to think first of the outcast and to regard others as equal to ourselves that we have all but lost sight of the ideal of individual excellence. We seem almost ashamed to admit that personal worth is, to its possessor, incomparably the most important thing on earth. We have been taught that meekness is a virtue, that ignorance and stupidity are not moral faults, that the gods look upon the vulgar with the same favor as upon the wise. As a result our morality has become a kind of petty clockwork way of behaving, the point of which appears to be nothing nobler than innocence. We have been so conditioned and enervated by the Beatitudes that we are hardly capable any longer even of understanding, much less appreciating, the truth that was so obvious to the pagan moralists: that what is worth having is not the common, but the uncommonly good. Socrates identified it with a condition of the soul, and much preferred death to the compromise of it. Aristotle called it intellectual virtue. The Stoics called it a life according to nature or reason. All of the moralists of classical antiquity called it *virtue*. Modern people also use this word, but with a debased meaning. It has been forgotten that virtue originally meant strength and superiority, and was correctly believed to be rare.

The attempt is made on these pages to reestablish philosophical ethics upon that foundation laid by the classical moralists of antiquity. Their ethical insights have never been surpassed and seldom even appreciated, for we see them all now through the distorting influence of religious ideas that were foreign to them. The history of philosophical ethics since the rise of Christianity has been a history of decline, finally degenerating into the verbal sparrings and lint picking of modern practitioners of the subject who imagine cleverness to be more precious than wisdom.

For much too long philosophers have been searching for ultimate moral distinctions that seem not to exist. They finally split into factions over the question of how such distinctions can be known. This eventually led to skepticism whether they can be known at all, the emotivists taking just that position. The fact that their dogmatic foes are themselves so divided suggests that there may indeed be no knowledge of this kind, and further, that perhaps there is nothing there to be known. It is the negative purpose of this book to make just that point, and to explain why. But that is not the end of ethics, as some would fear, but rather the beginning. The virtues await analysis, discussion, and defense. Socrates was quite certain that the inner person, or what one really is—in a word, virtue—is the most important object of philosophical reflection, and no one has raised any very convincing doubt about that. Why, then, not return to this?

Similarly, with respect to the nature of happiness, what is said here is, at best, only preliminary. Is it not time for philosophers to delve more deeply into this most important idea? Every important philosopher of antiquity after Socrates was profoundly concerned with it, but rather few since then have given it much thought, other than to try, in the case of the utilitarians, to erect some pointless rule of moral right and wrong upon the bare concept of it. Is there not, then, in this question alone enough to occupy philosophy for generations? There will, of course, be many answers, but from them we can hope to see emerge, once more, something that we see little hint of in the current disputations of philosophers, namely wisdom.

The influence of Aristotle in what follows will be obvious, especially in my description of the virtue of pride. It is significant that it took me thirty years and many readings of the *Nicomachaen Ethics* to appreciate the incomparable greatness of its author, this being due, I believe, less to my obtuseness than to the distorting influence of religious ideals, even in those who, like myself, imagine that they have rejected them.

This book grew out of my Gilbert Ryle lectures delivered at Trent University, in Ontario, in the fall of 1980. It is an elaboration upon what was said there, and while time has enabled me to enlarge upon the themes of those lectures, I have not otherwise modified them.

I am deeply grateful to Dr. Joseph Fletcher and Professor Jan Ludwig for reading my manuscript and helping me improve it in many ways, to Dr. Ray Perez for his translations of the passages from Aristotle, and to Hylda Taylor, Kim Fontana and Alice Erdman for editing it all and improving every page.

R.T.

ETHICS,
FAITH,
AND REASON

chapter 1

Introduction

A student of philosophy eventually notices something quite astonishing: The ancients, in spite of the fact that their contributions to moral philosophy are perhaps their most enduring philosophical achievements, seem to have given almost no thought to ethics as we understand the term. They discoursed at length on such things as friendship, the sources of happiness, the relative values of honor and wealth, and so on, but hardly ever got around to drawing the fundamental distinctions between what is right and what is wrong. Even Aristotle, whose *Nicomachean Ethics* is still admired as much as anything ever written on that subject, touches upon problems of right and wrong in an almost offhand manner. It is doubtful whether the ideas of *moral* right and wrong would even have made much sense to him. The subject of friendship, on the other hand, which modern practitioners of philosophical ethics hardly discuss at all, receives a lengthier treatment by Aristotle than any other subject in his book. Indeed, when one contemplates the works of the ancient classical moralists as a whole, it almost seems as if they were discoursing on something quite different from what their modern counterparts would regard as belonging to the subject matter of ethics.

The reason for this vast contrast between modern ethical philosophy and the ancient works from which it evolved is quite simple though rarely noticed and appreciated. The categories in which present day philosophers reflect upon ethics are the creations of a religious tradition with which the ancients were totally unfamiliar. Even those who today give little thought to religion are still, often unbeknown to themselves, locked into its categories. The result is that philosophers, with the exceptions of those few who take religion very seriously, are apt to talk nonsense the moment they address themselves to questions of ethics. They do not know that they are talking nonsense, because they find other philosophers who talk the same way, using such terms as duty, obligation, moral right and wrong, and so on. There is no way of checking what they say against any facts, and therefore they have no way of knowing whether what they are saying is true or even meaningful. Formulating their thought in terms that have a clear meaning in the context of religion, and no clear meaning outside that context, they raise questions that they cannot answer, precisely because answers to them do not exist. Religion first posed the questions and the answers. Philosophers abandoned those answers, but from the force of cultural tradition, kept the questions.

Thus contemporary philosophers of ethics think that such questions as these are quite fundamental: What is one's moral obligation? What ought we to do? What is our duty? What is the ultimate principle of moral right and wrong? And even when ethical questions are not posed in such general terms, it is nevertheless assumed that particular assertions of moral right and wrong make sense and can therefore be meaningfully asserted or denied. Thus even educated persons sometimes declare that such things as war, or abortion, or the violation of certain human rights, are "morally wrong," and they imagine that they have said something true and significant.

Educated people do not need to be told, however, that questions such as these have never been answered outside of religion. Perhaps we should say that they have been answered in numberless ways by numberless philosophers—which is, of course, another way of saying that they have not really been answered at all. They have merely been debated.

Why, then, if such questions are unanswerable, are they still treated as being so important? If there is no way of knowing the distinction between moral right and wrong, or if there is, in fact, no such distinction to be known, then why are such questions still disputed by educated people? If the philosophers of antiquity, preeminent in moral philosophy, did not, for the most part, think such questions worth discussing, then why do we?

The pages that follow constitute an answer to that question, but the outline of that answer is this: The ancients took ethics, in our sense of the term, for granted. They assumed, as many people tacitly assume still, that it consists simply of custom. The church, however, with its central idea of a supreme lawgiver, transformed that original, customary ethics into an ethics of duty to God. The modern age, more or less repudiating the idea of a divine lawgiver, has nevertheless tried to retain the ideas of moral right and wrong, not noticing that, in casting God aside, they have also abolished the conditions of meaningfulness for moral right and wrong as well.

That is the negative side of what follows. There is also a positive side. This may be summed up by saying that the long-neglected concept of virtue, which, in its original meaning, was the central concern of the ancient moralists, still merits the concern of modern ones.

chapter 2

The Ethics of Duty and the Ethics of Aspiration

Virtually everyone, philosophers included, supposes that ethics has always been primarily concerned with questions of moral right and wrong and the closely connected idea of moral obligation. Let us call this familiar concept *the ethics of duty.*

Ancient writers in philosophical ethics did not think that way at all. In fact they hardly touched upon the ideas of moral right and wrong, and their highest idea of obligation was political. They discoursed instead on human excellence or virtue, and on the closely associated ideas of pleasure, friendship, and the good life. When they talked about right and wrong at all, they usually had in mind nothing more than their own customs.

Let us call this ancient approach to ethics, in which the idea of individual excellence is so central, *the ethics of aspiration.*

THE TWO SOURCES OF ETHICS

Why, then, when our intellectual heritage is so overwhelmingly Greek in its roots and character, is there this enormous discrepancy between the two conceptions of ethics? Western civilization is certainly an achievement of immense importance in world history; and two basic ingredients of that achievement, both derived from the Greeks, are the scientific approach to the understanding of nature and the humanistic values of political life. Why, then, has the ethics of western civilization departed so radically from its origins in this same Greek culture?

The answer is essentially this: The Greeks derived their ethical ideals, and with them their philosophical approaches to ethics, from human nature, from a consideration of human needs and aspirations, and from their reflections upon political life. We, on the other hand, have derived ours from religion. And even though many persons, and certainly most philosophers, are no longer dominated by religious conviction in their thinking, our whole culture still views questions of ethics within the framework established by religion. We still assume that the basic ethical questions have to do with actions or policies, and that those questions reduce to moral rightness or permissibility.

Suppose, for example, one raises questions of the *ethics* of war, or euthanasia, or abortion, or truth telling. It is just assumed—is it not?—that the question being asked is whether the action or policy is morally right or wrong. That is, presumably, the ethical question. Nor is this simply a question whether such actions or policies are in keeping with our customs and traditions. That is not a question of ethics at all but of sociology. The waging of war, for example, is certainly customary, but the question whether it is morally permissible to wage war is not answered by that observation.

And so it is with respect to all the other questions that can be asked about things we do. We can ask whether they are advantageous, of frequent occurrence, permitted or forbidden by this group or that, and so on. The *ethical* question will always (it is thought) be something distinct from all these questions, namely, whether such things are or are not morally right. Ethics, it is said, is not concerned merely with what people in fact *do*, or *want* to do, or find it *advantageous* to do, or have been *taught* to do. Ethics is concerned with what people *morally ought* to do.

That the great moralists of classical antiquity did not discourse on ethics in this way, which seems so natural and even obvious to us, should certainly lead us to ask why they did not.

The answer to this question must begin with certain observations about Greek culture. While the ancient Greeks entertained beliefs of sorts about the gods, they had no priesthood and nothing like a church as we understand it. They had no thoughts of hell as a place of punishment for the wicked, nor of heaven as a place of reward for the good and the faithful. They believed in nature. Indeed their scientific, philosophical, and eventually even their ethical thinking was dominated by this idea; but they had no idea of the *super*natural. Even their gods were natural beings, with human thoughts and passions. Hence, while the idea of a lawgiver was as clear to the Greeks as to us, and while the gods were sometimes thought of as commanding and forbidding, and even sometimes as tyrannical, they were not thought of as supernatural, nor as omnipotent in the theological sense, nor even, usually, as outstandingly virtuous. These ideas are distinctively Christian, and the Christian religion had not yet made its appearance.

Of course there is much more to it than this; but the result, in any case, is that classical philosophical ethics, or the ethics of aspiration as we are calling it, is unqualifiedly humanistic. On the other hand, modern ethics, or the ethics of duty, is still essentially religious, even when divested of its religious presuppositions.

THE TWO DISTINCT CONCEPTIONS OF ETHICS

The ancient moralists ask: What is human excellence? What are the virtues? What is it to be an exemplary person, to stand apart from the common run? What is human fulfillment (*eudaemonia*), and how can one attain it?

Questions like these obviously overlap each other, but the question basic to all of them remains the same—namely, what is human excellence, and how is it achieved?

We, on the other hand, ask: What is morally right? What is morally forbidden? What is a person's moral duty or obligation? What does moral principle require of one?

These questions, too, overlap each other; but the important thing is to see how very different they are from the other questions, that is, the questions addressed by the ancients. While they asked, "What is human excellence?" we ask, "What is duty?" There may, of course, be some connection between the two questions, but it is not a very close one.

There in simplified terms is the basic and radical difference between two fundamental approaches to ethics, one of them humanistic and the other, as we shall see, religious.

Which approach, then, is the more rational or philosophical and the more fruitful?

Emphatically, it is the first, or humanistic one, in spite of the fact that it has, over the centuries, been virtually eclipsed by the other. The shift from the original ethics of aspiration to the ethics of duty did not result from any failure of the first; for the reflections of the ancient moralists are still intellectual achievements of towering greatness, and their power to inspire people to greatness and personal excellence has not been eroded by time. Approaching moral philosophy from this perspective, the ancient moralists created a literature that will inspire the world forever—or at least, will inspire those parts of the world that are able to free themselves from the religious background with its presumption of moral law.

On the other hand, modern philosophers, writing within the perspective of the ethics of duty and obligation, have managed to produce almost nothing that is not arid, trivial, and of no interest to anyone except themselves. Indeed, the ethics of duty cannot even be sustained independently of a religious framework, as we shall see. Contemporary writers in ethics, who blithely discourse upon moral right and wrong and moral obligation without any reference to religion, are really just weaving intellectual webs from thin air; which amounts to saying that they discourse without meaning. They imagine their utterances to be meaningful because they are made within an inherited framework, the framework of moral right and wrong. But they never attempt to justify that framework or to show that these basic distinctions have any meaning apart from religion. Instead, they simply take it as given. It is about time we took a closer look at that framework and its origins.

THE ECLIPSE OF THE ANCIENT IDEALS

We have noted that the moral perspective, referred to here as the ethics of aspiration and originated by pagan philosophers of antiquity, was over the course of time replaced by a different perspective called the ethics of duty, and it has been implied that this was due to religious influence. Just how this happened is obviously of immense importance, and is a much larger story than can be condensed into a few words. We can, however, sketch that story briefly here. It consists of two parts.

The first is that, with the rise of Christianity, the idea of a god (comprehended by faith) superseded the idea of nature (comprehended by reason). The consequences to ethics were overwhelming. Prior to the rise of Christianity, virtually everyone, including philosophers, had thought of right and wrong as corresponding to what is permitted and what is forbidden by tradition, custom, and law—in short, by rules that are of human origin whether written or unwritten. This whole realm of things, the realm of human enactment, was referred to by the Greeks as *nomos,* which we translate as *convention.* Of course there were exceptions to this, especially in the dramatic literature of the Greeks, where references are sometimes made to laws and principles of justice that transcend those of kings, as in the *Antigone.* No philosopher of standing took this idea seriously, however, and even Socrates' occasional references to the gods and to those non-human "voices" he felt bound to heed were essentially rhetorical and dramatic. They had no place in his philosophical dialectic.

With the advent of Christianity, however, the idea of the law of God, epitomized in Commandments vouchsafed through a priesthood, took on a new and awesome significance. Morality now went beyond obedience to merely human laws, customs, and traditions, and came to be thought of instead as obedience to divine law. Thus, what had hitherto been merely political and social obligation became distinguished, with the idea of a higher lawgiver, as moral obligation.

The second part of the story is that the ancient ideal of individual excellence was, quite amazingly, replaced by its opposite. That is to say, while the Greeks had upheld the ideal of excellence and nobility, which elevated its possessor *above* the common run of humanity, the Christians came upon the scene to announce that this common run, including the lowliest, was *itself* possessed of an excellence bestowed by the divine creator and actually surpassing anything reason could ever aspire to. People were declared to be the veritable images of God, just by virtue of their minimal humanity. They had, therefore, no greater individual excellence to aspire to, and their purpose became one of obligation, that is, obedience to God's will. Indeed, the new religion went even further in inverting the ancient ideal of individual excellence based upon reason by declaring the humble and the meek, that is, the *least* among us, to be the very salt of the earth and already blessed beyond measure. Therefore, they needed no special gifts or attainments of reason to possess this unique merit, according to this new point of view. They needed only to exist, and then, through the gift of faith, to learn what God expected of them.

SOME BASIC IDEAS OF THE ETHICS OF DUTY

Of course religion was not needed in order for human beings to form the basic idea of obligation and, with it, the ideas of right and wrong. One needs only to reflect upon how such terms first became meaningful to oneself in order to see this. Rather, the effect of religion was to transform these ordinary ideas, familiar to every culture, into the higher notions of *moral* obligation and *moral* right and wrong.

Thus, the ideas of right and wrong are basically and originally inseparable from the ideas of what things are *permitted* and what things *forbidden.* The idea of obligation, similarly, connotes that which is *required.* The very first notion any child has of something being *wrong* is simply that it is not allowed, by parent, teacher, or whomever. That is the sum and substance of its meaning for that child. Similarly for right. Something is *right* if it is permitted. If it is required that one do it, it is a "must," that is, obligatory. So it is, too, for primitive cultures. There are some things the members can do, others they cannot do, and still others they must do, these being enjoined by a tribal leader or, most often, by the members of the culture, as a group, expressing the power of inherited custom.

Wrong, then, essentially and originally means *forbidden. Right,* similarly, means *permitted.* And *obligatory* means *required.* Nor is it hard to see that these meanings are still inseparable from those most basic concepts of ethics. Thus, everyone would recognize something strange—at least in need of explanation—if told that it is permissible to do something that is conceded to be wrong, such as to fail to honor an obligation.

Who Are the Rule Makers?

Of course all this just raises another question already in the mind of any reflective reader. *Permitting, forbidding,* and *requiring* are themselves expressions of activities, or things that people do. We are therefore led to ask: Who is it that thus permits, forbids, or requires that certain things be done or not done?

There is a question, obvious to anyone and clearly fundamental to any inquiry into philosophical ethics, that, strangely, is seldom raised by philosophers themselves. If a given action is described as wrong and therefore forbidden, it seems the most obvious next question should be, Forbidden by whom?

The answer to this was taken for granted by the ancient moralists and, indeed, by virtually all the Greeks; up to a point it is just as obvious to us. The answer is *human beings,* meaning *people in general* or, more precisely, the people of a given culture if we are referring to the customs transmitted from one generation to another within such a culture. At another level the answer is *rulers and legislators,* when we are speaking of the actual laws of a political society.

Thus, for example, within a given culture the people, as a group, forbid stealing and express that prohibition by calling it wrong. On the other hand, it is the king or some comparable legislator who requires the payment of taxes or the giving of military service, and these are therefore described as obligatory.

Thus, as soon as a group of human beings begins to establish any kind of social life, it must live by certain rules, written or unwritten, as a necessary condition of living together. In this way arise the *customs* of a society, consisting of certain requirements and prohibitions on the part of its members. Of course these customs need not be thought of either as absolute principles, discovered by sages and philosophers, nor as authoritative commandments of any gods. They are simply the dos and don'ts that people perceive as necessary and desirable for social life. Common examples are the rules forbidding assault, homicide, theft, adultery, and so on. As primitive societies evolve into governed ones, the most important of such rules acquire the force of law, that is, they come to be enunciated and enforced by those who govern. Thus, when a king or tyrant declares homicide to be punishable, then *murder,* as a punishable offense, is raised from a mere taboo, forbidden by custom, to a crime, forbidden by law. In the same way other actions that would be basically inimicable to social life come under the prohibition of law—actions such as taking by stealth what another person already possesses, which comes to be called "theft," or doing the same by force, which comes to be called "robbery," or having carnal contact with a woman who is seen as "belonging" to another man, which comes to be called "adultery," and so on. All such actions are deemed *wrong,* in the sense that they are *forbidden,* this being, indeed, the original meaning of the word. In a similar way, other actions come to be deemed *right,* in the sense of being *permitted*; these include all those actions that are not forbidden. And still others come to be deemed *obligatory,* in the sense of being *required.* Thus, when a king, chieftain, tyrant, assembly, council (or whatever person or group actually holds the governing power) declares that certain taxes are to be paid, or that certain persons (men of a stated age, for example) are to bear arms in defense of the society, then these actions become *obligations,* that is, actions that are required not merely by custom but by law.

The laws are, however, like customs, obviously of purely human origin. And thus it is, in the last analysis, human beings who, at the level of custom and law, forbid, permit, and require those actions that come to be thought of as being either customarily or legally wrong, right, or obligatory. In the case of customs, the people in question are the people as a whole who, from one generation to another, transmit the basic and often unwritten rules by which that culture lives. In the case of laws, the people in question are not the people as a whole but rather those who hold the power of government, which always includes the power of making and enforcing laws.

Some Different Levels of Right and Wrong

The foregoing, fairly elementary reflections suggest another point that will already have occurred to philosophically reflective readers. We said that it would be very odd to speak of something as permissible even though wrong, or to say that someone is not required to do what is acknowledged to be obligatory. But of course this is not, as it stands, strictly true.

For example in some cultures, such as the predominantly Mormon culture of Utah, it is wrong to take the life of a fetus by abortion; yet it is permitted under the law. Similarly, infanticide was permitted by the Greeks, while it is considered by us to be wrong. And under the Nazi rule of Germany all sorts of abominations were permitted and even rewarded.

What such reflections show, of course, is not that the basic ethical ideas of right and wrong have no necessary connections with permission and prohibition but rather that there are different *levels* of right and wrong. Thus, what is forbidden by custom—abortion, in our example—may nevertheless be permitted by law. The breaking of a promise would be another example. Custom forbids it, but law does not except in certain clearly defined areas. Similarly, the infanticide practiced by the Greeks of antiquity did not violate their customs. If we say it was nevertheless wrong, we are only saying that it is forbidden by *our* ethical and legal rules. And the abominations practiced by the Nazis, with the approval of government, are forbidden by our rules and not, obviously, by theirs. To be sure, our rules may be "higher"—but what this means is something we shall need to consider later.

chapter 3

The Ideas of Right and Wrong

We need now to see more clearly how the basic ideas of right and wrong have arisen, and how, in our own tradition, the original and inspiring Greek ethics of aspiration came to be replaced by the now more familiar ethics of duty.

To do this, let us reconstruct imaginatively the origins and development of a civilized society. This type of imaginative reconstruction, first utilized in the opening books of Plato's *Republic,* and since then much used by the classical political philosophers, does not purport to be history. It is nevertheless a powerful intellectual tool for the clarification of certain basic philosophical ideas. We shall refer to the imaginary culture we are about to create as the Suekil, and to its members as the Suekils, suggesting by the backwards spelling that these people will turn out to be somewhat like us. This imaginative approach is intended to enable us to look at ourselves, as if in a mirror, but with the kind of detachment that imagination sometimes permits. In the imaginative account we are about to construct (with occasional commentary), we shall eventually find the division into two quite distinct conceptions of ethics, and we shall also come to understand how and why that bifurcation came about.

THE STORY OF THE SUEKILS

The Suekil people, let us imagine, had their beginnings in a wild and nameless plurality of human beings, living in geographical proximity to each other but without any social life at all. They subsisted by hunting and fishing, and thus had no need for cooperation among themselves beyond what was necessary for begetting and rearing children. If two or more such individuals met, they either passed each other in silence, or they simply retreated, avoiding each other. In any case, they did almost nothing together. Their relationship to each other was simply one of greater or lesser proximity; that is, they occupied the same area of land.

Obviously, there being no government, there were no laws among these people and, hence, no crimes. There were also no political obligations, such as the obligation to pay taxes. But more than that, there were no distinctions of right and wrong. For just as in the absence of laws nothing was unlawful, so also in the absence of customs or rules of any kind, even unwritten ones, nothing was taboo or forbidden. These people, depending on themselves alone, had no need for such distinctions, and they were as free from any constraints of law or morality as the birds of the air or the fish of the sea. Like these other creatures, they could break no law and do no wrong, and for the same reason: nothing was forbidden, either by law or custom. Neither justice nor morality had come into existence yet.

Comment: Here, at the beginning of our imaginary account, we have to resist the temptation to project into the Suekil culture certain more or less sophisticated ideas that we have derived from our own culture, ideas that seem to us elementary and obvious only because we are so used to them.

Thus, it would not be coherent to say: "Look, even if these people don't yet have any customs or laws, if one of them deliberately and wilfully kills another, then that's murder whether he knows it or not. The reason our laws forbid deliberate taking of human life is that such an act is murder. Laws do not *create* murders; they only enable a society to deal with them in case they are committed."

What is wrong with such a comment is that it confuses two distinct but overlapping things, namely homicide, which is the taking of human life, and murder, which is the unlawful taking of human life. That a life can be taken, deliberately and wilfully, in the absence of any prohibition of such action, is perfectly obvious. That such an act appears to us clearly condemnable is also obvious. And that, in any society, it ought to be punishable by law can also be granted. But to call such homicide *murder* is obviously to say something *more* than that it is an act of homicide. And what more is being said is, of course, that it is a crime, that is, a homicide punishable by law. And quite obviously no such crime can exist among the Suekils or anyplace else in the absence of such law.

For a similar, though slightly less obvious reason, it would be absurd to ascribe moral predicates, like right and wrong, to the actions of these people. Thus one cannot coherently say: "Look, even if these people have not reached the point of making laws and defining crimes, they certainly ought to be able to distinguish obvious cases of right or wrong. For example, it would be wrong if one of them should deliberately assault another, or steal from him, even if it were not punishable. Laws may create the distinction between lawful and unlawful, but they do not create the difference between right and wrong. On the contrary, it is because some things are already wrong that people make laws prohibiting them."

That kind of comment confuses two quite distinct things, namely the doing of something, and the doing of something in violation of custom or rule. That one person takes something that another person is holding in his hands is not, as such, a *wrong*, even though it may be resented. For it to be wrong there must be a rule, written or unwritten, that forbids it. Similarly, that a given man may cohabit with two or more female people, and perhaps call them all his wives, cannot be a wrong in the absence of any rule of monogamy, however deplorable it may appear in the eyes of those who have been taught to honor such a rule. That certain actions are done are facts. To say of such an action that it is done *and that it is wrong* is not to state *two* facts, but rather, to characterize one and the same fact. And what that characterization means, in case it means anything more than an expression of personal disapproval, is that the action in question is committed in violation of moral rule.

THE LEVELS OF RIGHT AND WRONG

It is at this point that we see again the importance of something touched upon before, that is, that there are various levels of right and wrong, and that they correspond to the several levels of rules. This is an important fact about ethics that will require more careful consideration later on, but it needs to be noted now in order to avoid serious confusion.

Thus there are rules, mostly unwritten and almost never embodied in law or elevated to the status of moral principles, that forbid such acts as picking one's teeth in public, using vulgar speech in polite company, giggling during solemn rituals, and so on. Violations of such rules are *wrongs*, but of a relatively trivial kind; they are essentially offenses to etiquette rather than to morality. An even lower order of wrongs comprises violations of rules governing the playing of games engaged in as mere pastimes. The violation of a rule of chess, for example, is neither an act of immorality nor an offense to etiquette, though it is wrong within the context of the game. Higher up are the violations of established custom, such as lying or failing to live up to a promise, even in circumstances where such actions are not punishable by law. One example might be declining to honor one's pledge of gifts to a church. Still another level of wrong is the violation of a criminal statute, that is, the commission of a crime. And still another level would be the violation of moral principle, even when such violation might be permitted or even required by custom and law—for example, putting innocent persons to death under the laws of a tyrannical government.

The point of noting this here—that is, of noting that there are many distinctions of right and wrong other than the distinction of moral right and wrong, and that some of these are of trivial significance in themselves—is to avoid being side-tracked by that observation. Its importance to ethics will emerge later on.

THE CONCEPT OF HARM OR INJURY

Returning now to a consideration of our imaginary Suekil people, whom we are thus far supposing to be without customs, laws, or government of any kind, we should note that, even in the absence of these, the possibility of harm or injury is perfectly real. No rules, customs, nor even social life are needed in order for someone to suffer injury. Rules are needed only for describing such injury as wrongful; they are no precondition of injury itself.

Thus, for example, if two such people meet, it is perfectly possible for one of them, instead of passing in silence or turning away, to assault or kill the other. Similarly, if one of them is carrying something—fruit, for example, or an animal intended for food—it is perfectly possible for the other to seize it either by stealth or by force. But it must still be borne in mind that such actions, though injurious to their victims, are no more unlawful, unjust, or immoral than they would be if done by one animal to another. A hawk that seizes a fish from the sea *kills* it, but does not *murder* it; and another hawk that seizes that fish from the talons of the first *takes* it, but does not *steal* it —for none of these things is forbidden. And exactly the same considerations apply to the people we are imagining. They can take from each other and thus injure each other, but they cannot steal or defraud; they can kill but not murder; they can go where they will but not trespass; and they can plunder but not rob. They are, in short, immune in what they do to any distinctions of justice or injustice, or of immorality. The conditions for these do not yet exist in the situation we are imagining.

Nor does it alter anything if we suppose the Suekils to be intelligent and rational beings like ourselves. The distinctions of right and wrong are not drawn by reason alone, nor does intelligence extract them from thin air. They result from the applications of reason to rules. *If* we think of the Suekils as intelligent and rational like ourselves, then we can hardly help supposing that they will, sooner or later, come to establish and inculcate certain customs and rules, written or unwritten, in order to lessen the chances of injury to themselves. No doubt that is true. But unless and until such rules or customs do somehow come about, then obviously nothing will be forbidden by custom or rule, and accordingly, nothing can be done in violation of them. Therefore the distinctions of right and wrong, just and unjust, cannot yet be made.

THE TRANSITION FROM MERE LIFE TO SOCIAL LIFE

Thus far we have before our imaginations a race of people but not a society. Let us now continue our account to find the ethical implications in the transition from a mere plurality of independent individuals to an elementary society.

The Suekils eventually begin to hunt together, to cooperate in erecting their dwellings and in defending the group against outside threat, to help each other in times of disaster, and gradually to create the concept of something "belonging" to someone and ideas as to how such ownership can be transferred.

Thus, the custom gradually evolves that any natural object that is useful will be considered to belong to that person who first finds and takes it. A fish is considered to belong to whoever catches it, or fruit to whoever finds and gathers it. Thus the idea of ownership, or *property,* is created. And with that arises the idea of a specific wrong, namely, *theft* and, thus, the idea of something forbidden or *wrong.* If someone seizes what another has first found and taken, then this latter person is no longer thought to be merely injured but *wrongfully* injured, that is, injured in violation of a custom or rule.

Other rules arise in much the same way among the Suekils. The commonest need these people have, for example, is for safety. Not much can be done to ensure safety from natural evils like disease, but at least they can take steps to reduce the likelihood that they will be assaulted by each other. We can imagine that a simple gesture evolves among these people as a sign of harmless intention. The gesture, let us suppose, consists of extending an open hand, as an indication that it holds no weapon. Now, if two Suekil people encounter each other, as a rule they no longer ignore, avoid, or attack each other. Instead, each extends an open, unthreatening hand; then they clasp hands briefly, the simple ritual conveying to each, in the clearest manner imaginable, that the other is not going to attack him.

Thus another rule arises, unwritten to be sure, but a rule nonetheless and an important one, clearly understood by all. And it is a rule that, like any other, can be violated. Thereafter if two Suekil people meet, extend open palms, shake hands, and one of them assaults the other (perhaps with a knife concealed in the other hand), the victim of this assault is not only injured but *wrongfully* injured, or injured in violation of established rule.

Comment: It is not hard to see here the beginnings of right and wrong or, in other words, the emergence of ethics. We need only to think of people living together, not as a mere assemblage, but as a society, cooperating in the pursuit of common goals. Customs, or unwritten but shared rules, are needed for this, and with the emergence of such customs there arises the possibility of violating custom or doing what is forbidden. Such violation constitutes the basic and original idea of a wrong.

Here it is worthwhile to note that there is no suggestion, in this imaginative account, that human beings ever did in fact join into societies after an initial state of isolation from each other, though this is of course perfectly possible. It does not matter, for our purposes, whether that ever happened or not; and it may very well be true that human beings, as long as they have existed at all, have lived in societies. Indeed, the picture of rational human beings living in proximity to each other but with no social organization may be inherently absurd from the standpoint of history and anthropology. But that is not the point. For we are trying, through this imaginative exercise, to understand the basis of the familiar distinctions between right and wrong, just and unjust. We are not offering a historical or anthropological account of the origins of societies. We have thus far supposed that our imaginary people have been converted from a mere multitude to a society, through cooperation and the emergence of customs governing their behavior towards each other, in order to show how customs give rise to the distinction between what is and what is not allowable, and thus, to the distinction between right and wrong.

THE TRANSITION FROM AN UNGOVERNED TO A GOVERNED SOCIETY

Let us now return to the simple society we were imagining, and contemplate its further development.

Eventually there arises among the Suekil people some forceful person who takes upon *himself* the creation of rules and from time to time announces these to the rest. Thus, while the people still transmit inherited rules and customs from one generation to the next, they now acquire a new and more specific source of particular rules, namely, an identifiable lawgiver. Either out of fear or awe for this person, the people heed these specific rules and give their source the name "Chief," or some other title indicating the unique role of rulemaker. With this development there arises, on top of the basic distinction of right and wrong created by customs, the idea of *laws*; and with this, the idea of the *violation* of law; and with this the idea of a *crime*. There also emerges the concept of justice in its legal sense.

Comment: A crime is the breach not merely of a custom but of a law. But for a law to be broken, it must exist; and for a law to exist, there must be a lawgiver. And this is precisely what we are now supposing with respect to our Suekil people. We are thinking of them not merely as cooperating, and thus as belonging to a rudimentary society, but as governed, and thus belonging to a rudimentary *polis,* commonwealth, or nation. As this commonwealth develops under the laws emanating from that person or those persons who govern, so also do the distinctions of justice and injustice and of obligation become more refined. Those things that come to be required by the laws, such as payment of taxes and cooperation in the common defense, come to be thought of as *obligations.* Those that come to be forbidden by the laws, such as fraud, trespass, bigamous marriage, poaching, and so on, come to be thought of as *crimes.* And *justice,* which before had no meaning other than that derived from custom, now comes to mean respect for these laws and injustice the disregard of them.

We now have before us, in the barest outline, the picture of how a mere assemblage of people becomes a society through the development of customs and, with these, of the idea of things that are forbidden; and how a simple primitive society, whose members cooperate by adherence to custom, becomes a *governed* society, or commonwealth, through the development of laws emanating from one or more lawmakers.

What, then, has our simple imaginative sketch of the Suekil culture illustrated so far? Not a great deal; but what has emerged has immense significance as the foundation for the overwhelmingly important philosophical ideas that will be developed later. Indeed, it is probably just because these ideas are so simple and obvious that they tend to be overlooked by writers and teachers of ethics. Such persons assume that the concepts of right, wrong, and obligation just stand by themselves, awaiting analysis, as though their meanings had no roots in the customs and rules of human origin. What we have before us are the basic ideas of (1) right and wrong that apply to those actions permitted or forbidden by custom, and (2) of justice and injustice that apply to those actions or policies that are in accordance with or in violation of the commands of lawmakers. We also have the clear idea of injury, and the correlative idea of benefit, but as we have noted, those ideas have been there from the beginning. Neither customs nor laws nor indeed anything other than nature itself was ever needed to give content to these ideas. A person, just like an animal, can be injured by a falling branch or by lightning, and neither customs nor laws are necessary for such occurrences. Similarly, one can be benefited by weather, over which we have no influence, or by a bounty of food, even when this is not a product of human industry. So again, neither customs nor laws are needed for these.

Thus while the concepts of right and wrong, and of justice and injustice, presuppose customs and other rules made by human beings, those of good and bad, of benefit and injury, do not. Everything that lives is susceptible to injury or benefit, and this would be no less true if human beings had never existed.

One might indeed note, at this point, that contemporary ideas of right and wrong, and of justice and injustice, are certainly richer and more profound than what we have been considering. And that is certainly true. Few people would be content to regard the adherence to or violation of mere customs as equivalent to right and wrong, even when the customs in question happen to be their own. Customs vary, and some are not only primitive but pernicious in themselves, from which it of course appears doubtful that right and wrong can be defined in terms of them. Similarly, there has to be more to the distinction between justice and injustice than obedience to or violation of human laws. Laws can emanate from tyrants, and hence be unjust; from which it surely follows that justice and injustice cannot be defined in terms of those laws.

The point is of course well taken and has already been touched on, but it is still premature. We have yet to see how the ideas of *moral* right and wrong or the ideas of rational and natural justice and injustice arise, and until we do, we should not suppose that we already understand them.

chapter 4

The Emergence of Philosophy and Religion

Let us now take the next step and suppose this Suekil society is flourishing. The emergence of custom has enabled its members to survive and cooperate, thereby, quite literally, *accustoming* them to what can and what cannot be done. The subsequent emergence of acknowledged rulers and their laws has enabled the society as a whole to survive and, given the right conditions, to thrive. We shall now imagine that it moves to the next stage, that is, to that of a genuinely civilized culture. Nature bountifully supplies this young and vigorous culture; its security is not so constantly threatened as to sap its energies; and perhaps as the result of a vast class of slave laborers, leisure becomes possible to some, and learning and the arts, which were hitherto unknown, come into existence. People no longer limit themselves to what is useful. Some of them want to know what is—perhaps uselessly—true. Thus arise the beginnings of intellectual pursuit. They no longer create buildings and weapons and pots just to meet their basic needs; some of them try to create things of this sort that will be beautiful. The arts arise. They no longer apply measurements and rules of thumb concerning angles and distances merely to create structures and boundaries. They try to understand the rules themselves. Mathematics and geometrical science have their beginnings. They develop spoken and written language, not only to communicate with each other, but to reach for deeper and more lasting meanings. Literature, drama, and the search for wisdom, which we call philosophy, are born.

The Suekil philosophers are profoundly curious about the world, about the behavior of nature, the seasons, living things, the phenomena of weather, the heavens—everything that surrounds them. Unlike other ancient cultures, which for the most part have sought answers to all such questions in magic or from priests, these philosophers propound theories and try, with such means as they have, to check them against what they actually observe. Thus is born the rational and disinterested search for truth.

THE TWO KINDS OF TRUTH

Eventually some of these philosophers declare that there are two quite different kinds of truths, namely, those that result from human enactment and those that do not. The latter, they say, are those truths that are simply discovered, while the former are those that are made, at least originally. Thus, for example, it is *discovered* that all people are mortal, that some are male and some female, that fire burns, that stones fall earthward, and so on. These things are not true because someone has declared that this is how things should be. They are just facts that are found, not made.

Certain other facts, on the other hand, though incontestably true, are declared by the Suekil philosophers to be different from the kinds of facts just noted. Thus, such facts as that some people are slaves and others free, or that some are married and others not, or that one man is king and another subject, or that people make sacrifices to the gods in this way or that, or that certain places and days are sacred or holy; are *not* simply discovered. They are things that someone has, at some time or another, *made* true. They are thus facts made, not facts merely found.

Thus, the philosophers point out, a person is born male, or female, as the case may be; he or she does not become such by declaration or ceremony. But no one is born a magistrate or a married person. Someone is made such by the actions of others. And one is similarly made wealthy, or a criminal, or the inheritor of an estate, by certain things that he or she and others do.

Having made this fairly elementary distinction, the philosophers among the Suekils raise the following significant question: What about the distinction between right and wrong? Is it, like the difference between round and square, one that is simply found? Or is it like that between slave and free person, one that is made?

Similarly, what about the distinction between just and unjust? Are some things simply *seen* to be unjust, the way some things are seen to be large or small? Or should we say that some things are *deemed* unjust, the way someone is deemed or declared to be the owner of a given ring, or horse, or whatever?

Thus two very distinct schools of moral philosophy arise among these people. The one school declares that the ultimate principles of morality and justice are as clear and invariable as those of mathematics or any science, that they are in no way relative to the varying declarations of people but discovered to be the same everywhere by the application of human reason, and that while the customs and laws of people may vary from one culture to the next, the underlying principles of justice do not.

The other school declares that these principles result, every one of them, from human enactment, and they are nothing more than the distillations of customs and laws, all of which are of human fabrication. There is, therefore, nothing in this realm for philosophers to *discover* other than the manner in which such customs and laws have gradually come into being.

Comment: This distinction between two kinds of truth is easily grasped and quite obviously significant; yet strangely, it is rarely appreciated by present-day thinkers. It is somehow thought sufficient to distinguish between the true and the false, without further distinguishing between things that are made true by human beings, which could, accordingly, have been made false, and those that are true quite independently of anything that anyone does or can do about them. It would be true, for example, that the earth is round and that fire burns even if there had never been a single human being in the world. Nor can all the laws, customs, declarations, and decrees of even the most powerful lawgivers alter the fact that some people are male, others female. On the other hand, rather little is needed to render it true that a given person is married, or is a slave, or a magistrate and truths of this sort, though unmistakably truths, can as easily be made false. What human beings have done can often be undone; and, even more significantly, they might not have done in the first place.

This important distinction did not escape the penetrating thought of the ancient moralists of history, however sadly it has been neglected by their descendants. We shall return to it later, and discover its far-reaching consequences.

SPECULATIONS ON VIRTUE

There is, however, another and quite different line of thought that we can imagine the Suekil philosophers to pursue. We can suppose that, having worked out the basic principles of mathematics and geometry and having carried forth their speculations on nature and the cosmos, they now turn their attention to the following question: If some things are good and some bad, then what is a good human being? They note that things are, generally speaking, good because they are good *for* something. Thus, a good knife is good for cutting, a good garment for keeping oneself warm, and so on. Similarly, with people: A good physician is good for healing, a good musician for making music, and so on. What, then, is a good *person*? What is human excellence? What makes some persons better than others? What, in short, is virtue? All of which questions presuppose that human beings exist *for* something or other, and the task of the philosophers will be to find out what this is.

Comment: These are good questions, and the answers that moralists of the Suekil culture will give them will constitute the moral philosophy of these people. They are questions that invite thought and reflection, which means they are rational questions. Answers to them will not be sought by turning to priests, to alleged truths vouchsafed from another realm, or to sacred tablets or books, nor will they be sought through magic. The various answers that gain considerable followings will identify the various "schools" of moral philosophy, each with some founder or exemplary teacher whose reflections seem reasonable to the minds of his followers.

What is to be noted about this kind of question is that it does *not* encompass any particular theory about moral right and wrong. A reflective, philosophical member of the Suekil culture, engrossed in the question of the nature of human goodness, might very naturally assume that the distinction between right and wrong is simply one created by custom, and that customs are in the last analysis the creation of his ancestors. In other words, he can suppose *right* to mean "what is permitted by custom and law," and *wrong* to mean what is similarly forbidden. *Obligatory* can be similarly understood, as that which is required—required by the king, for example, or by his laws. No such suppositions, so seemingly in keeping with common sense, would have much effect upon the other, quite different question of moral philosophy that we suppose thinkers of this culture to be concerned with, namely the question: What is human excellence, or virtue?

THE IMPACT OF RELIGION

We shall now sketch the remaining stages in the evolution of ethics among these imaginary people.

The first stage results from the amalgamation of this highly civilized culture with another whose traditions are totally different. This other culture, whose members we shall call the Rehto people, we can suppose to be as old as the Suekil civilization, but very different in its intellectual traditions. The Rehto people originated in a different part of the world altogether, but as the Suekil culture gradually declined, weakened by wars, that of the Rehto's flourished, and the two eventually became blended together to become the foundation of great civilizations that followed.

Thus, we imagine the Rehtos to turn for answers to their questions about the world, not to philosophers as do the Suekils, but to a long-established priesthood, and to a sacred literature that has accumulated over many generations at the hands of this priesthood. They come to believe that the world and everything in it was made by the gods, thereby putting curiosity to rest. All the great episodes of history—the wars, floods, and the rise and fall of nations—they declare to have come about under the guidance of these gods and their chosen, human emissaries. All living things are represented as having been made by the gods, including, of course, people; but people have a unique relationship to those gods, they claim, not shared by other creatures. This relationship they describe by saying that people are very much like the gods, veritable copies of them, and are therefore favored by them over all the other creatures they have made. From the same claim, they infer that all other living things are profoundly inferior and have no role in the divine plan other than to be used by the human duplicates of the gods.

It is in this fashion that the Rehtos answer every question, large or small, by reference to the works of the gods. Of course no attempt is ever made to prove that any of these things are true, other than to cite venerable authorities who have declared them to be true, or who have written them down as true, such writings then being added to the literature, deemed sacred, upon which the Rehto culture rests. All these things come to be believed, even without proof, or indeed, without evidence, beyond what is declared by the priesthood. The Rehto people believe that their identity and survival as a nation depend upon their allegiance to their traditions and the teachings contained in their books as interpreted and proclaimed by their priests.

THE EMERGENCE OF DIVINE LAW

In addition to explaining everything about the world, its origin and its history, the gods of the Rehtos have another role whose importance far exceeds even the explanatory one. *They are lawgivers.* The gods enunciate, through the priesthood, everything that is expected of the people, encompassing virtually every aspect of life. From these laws, the people learn how the gods are to be worshiped, what days shall be set aside as holy, what rules shall govern marriage and the rearing of children, how they are to treat their neighbors and their property, and so on. They learn all the things they are commanded by the gods to do and, especially, all the things they are forbidden to do. The most important of these commands are memorized in childhood, and frequently and ceremoniously repeated for the rest of their lives. To disregard or violate them, the people are taught, is far more serious than violating the laws of any earthly rulers, and the consequences of such violation, accordingly, far more grave.

Eventually one of the Rehto priests breaks away from the others, declaring himself to have an even closer kinship to the gods than any of them can claim, and he rests the authority of his own declarations upon that unique relationship. He proclaims that those who have hitherto always been regarded as the least significant of people—the poor, the weak, the ignorant and stupid—are, on the contrary, the very most important people on earth and are most favored by the gods! These seemingly inferior masses, he says, will, contrary to everyone else's and even their own expectations, end up with everything. He compares them to gold and precious gems, says they are the leavening of the whole world, without which no good thing can happen, and declares that someday the gods will establish on earth a kingdom like their own, with the meek and the humble at its head. The masses of the weak and dispossessed, hearing all these strange new teachings, gather around this new priest, echoing his claims against the opposition of the powerful traditional priesthood and, after he has been put to death by his rivals, they all maintain that he was never actually put to death at all, but lives on, and will someday return to his followers to establish the promised kingdom.

THE NEW ETHICS

As the culture of the Suekil people, which we have described, declines and that of the Rehto people first infiltrates and then virtually overwhelms it, philosophers, responding to both influences, devise a quite new conception of ethics, differing from their traditional conceptions in two significant ways.

First of all, they entirely abandon the idea that human excellence rests upon any natural human purpose or function. In fact they cease talking about human excellence or virtue altogether, with its connotations of the natural superiority of some over others. Real virtue, they say, does not consist of the exercise of any merely natural human ability, such as intelligence, but rather, of something that is within the reach of all, even the ignorant and forsaken—namely, of *belief* in the person and teachings of the holy man who has become identified with the new doctrines. Since this is available to all, there is no longer any merit in supposing that one person can be, in any ordinary sense, better than others. The only true strength and excellence is that of the weak and inferior, for that is the goodness approved by the gods. The weak are the truly strong, the ignorant most wise, and the impoverished and hopeless, most blessed.

And secondly, they declare that the distinctions of right and wrong, justice and injustice are, as had always been maintained, distinctions established by rules and laws. But the rules and laws made by human beings are no longer to be considered the highest ones. There are laws that take priority over all of these, even over the laws of kings and the rules of conduct long thought to have their origins in reason. These are the laws enunciated by the gods and transmitted through the literature of the Rehtos and their priesthood. Customs, they say, create distinctions of right and wrong only at the human level, and can therefore sometimes be disregarded, inasmuch as they rest upon merely human authority. The laws of kings and human legislators, too, create only relative distinctions of justice, since such legislators have at best nothing more than human reason to guide them. The laws of the gods, however, since they exceed in their source and authority everything human, establish the absolute and changeless distinctions of true justice, valid for all persons everywhere. What the gods declare to be right is indeed right, even when it is repugnant to what is declared to be right by the wisest philosophers or the greatest of kings. And similarly, what is declared to be wrong is in fact wrong, absolutely.

Thus was the philosophy and wisdom of the ancient Suekil moralists overwhelmed, so that for all practical purposes it entirely disappeared, to be known henceforth only to scholars and antiquarians. It was no longer a significant part of the thinking even of highly cultured and educated people who, like the masses of ignorant outcasts, turned instead to the new teachings and embraced these ideas of morality and duties to the gods. They were, however, quick to make certain basic and necessary modifications in those teachings, especially as they related to the vanity of power and wealth. What was retained was the claim, as old as the Rehto culture itself but unknown to the ancient Suekils, that there are laws higher than those of any king or other human legislator, binding on all the world, and hence, that there is an absolute and changeless distinction between right and wrong, a distinction clearly implied in the claim that these laws come, not from human beings, but from the gods.

THE EMERGENCE OF PHILOSOPHICAL ETHICS

The culture of the people we are imagining thus became an amalgamation of two very different cultures. From the Suekils they derived their science, philosophy, and political ideas, and from the Rehtos their religious ideas, their idea of divine laws and of moral right and wrong.

Philosophy and science, which rested upon reason, were never able to make any lasting alliance with religion, however, as the latter inclined towards the repudiation of reason in favor of faith. Therefore philosophy, when it was finally able to reassert itself against the claims of religion, discarded the idea of divine lawgivers, and sought instead to base morality upon human reason and intelligence.

But then a very strange thing happened. The moral philosophers, instead of returning to the moral ideals of the Suekils, who were their philosophical ancestors, and to the ideals of human excellence and fulfillment, turned instead to the ideas of moral right and wrong inherited from the Rehtos! Indeed, the concepts themselves of the ancient moralists came to be so diluted with ideas inherited from religion that even the philosophers lost sight of their original meanings. The concept of virtue, for example, which had originally been that of strength and superiority that sets its possessor above the rank and file of people, came instead to have almost the opposite meaning. The virtuous came to be thought of not as the bold and heroic but as the meek and common who excelled in nothing. In the same way, the moral philosophers of the new age abandoned altogether the idea of intellectual virtue, which bestowed upon its possessor qualities that made him better than the ignorant, declaring, in keeping with the religious morality, that no one can really be any *better* than anyone else, that the masses of stupid and uncouth people have the same moral worth as their opposites and are therefore entitled to the same treatment. And continuing in the same direction, these new moral philosophers virtually abandoned the idea of the fulfillment of function as the key to well-being, replacing it with a debased concept of happiness, which they identified with pleasant feelings and declared to be within the reach even of the vulgar and common. Thus were the ancient moral ideals lost to the later generations of philosophers, to say nothing of their total disappearance from the minds of everyone else. The very terms in which those ancient ideals had been described either ceased to be meaningful or, what was more common, came to have different and often almost opposite meanings attached to them.

What concepts, then, remained for the modern philosophical moralists? The concepts of *right* and *wrong* remained though not, to be sure, in the way these had been understood by the ancient Suekils, as ideas derived from the rules of custom and law. Instead, these became the ideas of *moral* right and wrong, originally derived from the laws claimed by the Rehtos to be enunciated by the gods but now divested, in the minds of the philosophers, from that source. Thus the modern philosophers no longer gave much thought to divine laws, declaring these to be the province not of reason but of faith. Instead they spoke of "moral" laws, and a kind of universal justice, resting their conviction in the reality of moral right and wrong upon their belief that such laws, and such justice, must actually exist. This latter, of course, they had a very difficult time proving, since they could point to no lawgivers as the sources of these alleged laws and could find in nature nothing resembling the laws upon which distinctions of justice had always been made. Faced with this difficulty, they finally started treating moral right and wrong as properties of actions *themselves* and were not particularly bothered by the fact that such properties seemed not only to be quite invisible, but differently interpreted by virtually every philosopher who discoursed upon them. Their thinking was that there somehow *had* to be such a distinction between moral right and wrong, superior to the distinctions created by human custom and law, for otherwise, they thought, they would have nothing to talk about. But since there appear to be no lawmakers superior to those that are human, then, they said, we must suppose that moral right and wrong are just part of the fabric of nature itself, however inherently implausible this bizarre supposition may seem. Having persuaded themselves of this, it was of course not difficult to speak of the same nature as creating the ultimate distinctions of justice, a role that the religious had once assigned to the gods.

Moral philosophy, in short, cut itself adrift from *both* of the traditions from which it had emerged, and sundered from these, it became completely empty of content. It took from the religious tradition, or the culture of the Rehtos, the concepts of moral right and wrong but shed what had been the foundation of those concepts, namely, divine law. And it took from the philosophical and scientific tradition of the Suekils the concepts of nature and reason but shed the ideals of human excellence and well-being that had rested on them. The attempt was made to weld together two things that did not mix at all, namely, reason on the one hand and moral right and wrong on the other. Bogged down in the attempt to join these, moral philosophy became empty of real content, and its practitioners finally found that they had nothing to say to anyone except each other. Talking to each other, they discoursed entirely on concepts and meanings that they derived either from cultivated usage or from thin air.

Summary comment: One can hardly fail to see a resemblance between the imaginary account just given and the evolution of ethical thought in our own culture. That was, in fact, the whole point of the story. Of course, the imaginary sketch does not pretend to be even a rough intellectual or cultural history, for certainly things are not as simple as there suggested. It is, nevertheless, useful in exposing certain very important themes. The sketch given is based upon imagination rather than fact precisely to avoid the criticism that it is a distortion of fact. What is avowedly imaginative can never be a distortion of anything. We are not here concerned with the details of intellectual history, nor with the diverse themes expressed in our very complex religious and philosophical background. We are concerned instead with some very large and important ideas, and we are trying to give some account of how they come to be meaningful.

What has been presented in an imaginative and oversimplified sketch is intended to suggest how the moral philosophy of western civilization has changed over the centuries under the joint influence of reason and religion, with the further suggestion that this change has been very much for the worse.

In the pages that follow we shall see what has happened to the moral ideas, not of some imaginary people, but of our own culture. In this overwhelmingly important aspect of our culture—that is to say, in our ethical thinking—we have simply gone downhill, not for generations but for two millennia. Extolling reason, philosophers nevertheless cling to basic ideas derived from religion, at the same time repudiating the religious framework that gives those ideas meaning. And, thus caught up in concepts that are really quite foreign to reason, particularly the ideas of moral right and wrong, they have almost entirely lost sight of the original ideas of ethics, which are *not* foreign to reason but the very fruit of it—particularly the ideas of virtue and happiness.

chapter 5

Greek Ethical Ideals

Western civilization lost something very precious when the ethical ideals of the Greeks were eclipsed by religious ones, especially by those of the Christian church. We need to get before us a clear picture of what those ancient ideals were.

We shall not attempt a history of ancient Greek ethics. This would not only be too large a task, it would also defeat our purpose, for we would lose sight of the very ideas we are seeking. They would have become buried in the particular ideas and arguments of the various philosophers.

What we shall do is consider the main currents of the ethical thought of the Greeks, illustrating them in ways that seem apt but with no attempt at comprehensiveness.

THE THREE BASIC IDEAS

Greek moralists were primarily concerned with two ideas, virtue and happiness. A third idea, justice, was also important, but less so than these first two, and the idea of duty (other than political) or, what amounts to much the same thing, moral obligation played almost no part at all in their thinking.

They thought of virtue not simply as rectitude in one's dealings with others and certainly not as mere kindness, but rather, as a kind of skill. And they thought of happiness not as a feeling but as a kind of basic fulfillment. We get some notion of the corruption both ideas have undergone when we realize that, in the minds of many, "virtue" has come to mean mere innocence or, worse yet, sexual purity, while "happiness" has, to the same persons, come to be equated with bountiful possession or, even worse, pleasure.

Let us try to recapture the older and nobler associations of these two ideas, beginning first with virtue.

The Ancient Idea of Virtue

The most common idea of virtue among the Greeks was that it represented *any* useful and desirable art, skill, or capacity. Thus, they thought, there are many virtues just as there are many arts or skills. There is the virtue of the soldier, that of the horseman, that of the pilot, the physician—whatever. A *good physician,* for example, is one who is skilled in the art of healing. A *good soldier* is one who is skilled in warfare. A *good ruler* is one skilled in the art of statecraft. The *virtues* of such people are, then, precisely those skills—their abilities to do well whatever it is that they do.

Virtue was, from the start, associated with excellence, with what stands out as especially good. One becomes virtuous, not by becoming like others but the very opposite. He comes to be *unlike* others in his ability to do exceptionally *well* what they are, at best, merely able to *do.*

Nor did the Greeks limit the concept of virtue to human excellence. Anything that has a use, they thought, also has a virtue—and of course they were correct in this given their conception of virtue. Thus, just as you can speak of a good physician (someone who is skilled at healing the sick), so also you can speak of a good knife (one that cuts well), a good ship (one that is sturdy and handles well), a good house (one that fulfills the purpose for which a house is built), and so on. The idea of virtue was one of appraisal, establishing important distinctions of better and worse, whether with reference to persons or to anything else.

Next it should be noticed that for the ancient moralists the idea of virtue had an essential connection with that of *function.* Different persons and things have different functions, which they can fulfill either well or ill. It is, for example, the function of a physician to heal, the function of a ruler to govern, of a lawmaker to legislate, and so on. Similarly, it is the function of a knife to cut, of a house to shelter, and so on. And a thing is evaluated as *good* or *bad* according to how well it fulfills its function. A good pilot, for example, is one who not only guides a ship in and out of the harbor, but one who performs this function with skill. A physician is someone who treats the sick and the wounded, but one is not a good physician if a very considerable number of these get worse or die. A good physician is thus one who fulfills this function skillfully and effectively, one who can be counted on to restore his patients to health.

All this is fairly straightforward, perhaps even banal, and it is not immediately obvious what virtue, in this sense, has to do with ethics. But notice now the question that is certain to arise in the mind of a philosopher or indeed of anyone who is reflective, *What is a good person?*

Here is a question that is not only important, but of supreme importance to ethics. And we seem to have before us the philosophical formula for answering it. For if the goodness of anything is to be found by determining how well it fulfills its function, then we need only to consider the particular function of a human being in order to discover the nature of human goodness.

Here, of course, we are no longer asking about the function of this or that person in his role of soldier, physician, or whatever. We already know these things. We are instead asking about the function of a person, just considered as a person. And this amounts to asking what it is that distinguishes a person from anything else, or what is the particular excellence of persons that sets them apart from other living things.

We share life, sense, and appetite with other beings. It therefore cannot be our function as persons merely to live, to enjoy, or to satisfy our wants. But there is something that is uniquely ours and that is the capacity for thought and reason. We share this with no other earthly beings. It is clearly this capacity that constitutes our particular excellence, setting us apart from everything else in the world.

From this we can see at once what a *good* person is. This is not just someone who thinks and reasons but one who thinks and reasons outstandingly well. This is, in the fullest and most praiseworthy sense, a rational being, guided by reason and intelligence in everything, in the understanding of the world and of himself, and in the guidance of conduct. Human goodness or virtue turns out to be not mere good will, and certainly not innocence, but the cultivation of a fully rational life at a level which rather few can ever hope to attain.

This is essentially the way in which the ideal of the rational life and the activity of rational inquiry, generally, became a basic part of our intellectual and cultural heritage. No civilization prior to the Greeks so exalted reason. It is still an ideal, but it has not been without competitors, the most obvious being the ideal of faith to which reason is always directly opposed. But of this, more later.

Happiness

The second idea that was important to the ancient moralists was, as noted, that of happiness. Their word was *eudaimonia,* which means, literally, having a good demon. The sense of this is in some ways apt, for it suggests a kind of supreme good fortune, of the sort that might be thought of as a bestowal.

When these philosophers asked what happiness is, they were trying to ascertain the nature of a genuinely meaningful and fulfilling life. Implicit in this is, of course, another question, How can one attain it?

These moralists were not just idly looking for a definition of the word, "happiness," nor were they particularly interested in knowing what the average run of people are content to consider a happy life. It seemed clear to them that life is susceptible of great and lasting significance and, also, that it can be utterly wasted. Genuine happiness is rare, and its attainment difficult. Moreover, they noted, it is quite common for someone to get everything he wants and nevertheless live a totally wasted life. Consider the powerful tyrant. He has, in a sense, everything he wants; he is subject to no law but his own, lives in visible splendor, and is bowed down to by everyone. Yet his life seems to be squandered in the pursuit of specious, meaningless things or, worse, of positive evils. He has no good life, no real sense of fulfillment, no happiness, but like a man starving for food and drink, is constantly expending his energies in the pursuit of pleasures, new possessions, new triumphs.

The example is a good one because most people, without thinking much about it, would consider the amassing of wealth and power to be worthwhile ends, and this the powerful tyrant has certainly succeeded in doing. He is the envy of all. But if we consider him more closely, we find that in his constant desperation to satisfy his appetites he only falls victim to new ones and never does find the fulfillment he so ineptly seeks. He has, then, missed the mark. And so, it seemed to the wisest moralists, has just about everyone else. Happiness is something everyone seeks, yet few ever find. Some—indeed most—have no clear idea of its real nature, so they do not know what to aim for. They wander from the path of happiness because they do not know where they are supposed to be going. Others, though they may have a better idea of what a truly meaningful and fulfilling life would be, do not know how to get it; or else they are distracted by other pursuits, such as the pursuit of pleasure, or honor, or reputation, and such things.

It seemed clear to these philosophers that we need to know what this elusive happiness really is; and finally, knowing that, we need to know how it is attained.

And they were right. Both are good questions. Indeed, there are no better or more important questions that one can consider. And if moral philosophy is, in part, the quest for answers to these questions, then there is probably nothing better to devote oneself to than moral philosophy.

Justice

If the ancient moralists were so concerned with the ideas of virtue and happiness, then what of the idea of justice, which seems to us so basic to ethics?

Justice, and the distinctions of right and wrong generally, were not so important to the classical moralists, for reasons already suggested. Most people thought of justice as consisting of nothing more than the conventional practices of social life. The Greek word *ethnos* meant simply, "people like us." Our word *ethnic,* which is derived from it, preserves exactly that meaning. *Ethos,* from which we get *ethics,* originally meant simply *habit,* or the habitual or customary practices of "people like us." It consisted, in other words, of the customs and practices of a given culture—Athenian, or Persian, or Spartan, or whatever. There was, prior to Socrates, no important thinker who suggested that there could be any kind of absolute or changeless justice, independent of the customary usages gradually fabricated by this culture or that. This idea simply had not occurred to people.

Gradually these three ideas—virtue, happiness, and justice—came to be closely connected in ancient moral philosophy, so that most moralists maintained, in one way or another, that only the just are happy and that, sometimes contrary to appearances, a just person cannot fail to be "happy," that is, to possess a life that is both good and beautiful. And these two ideas, in turn, were easily linked to that of virtue, so that the truly just, and hence happy person, was also the examplar of virtue, in the sense of human excellence. Since, moreover, virtue was still associated in the minds of moralists with skill or art, the emphasis of early moral philosophy was, most refreshingly, on the *art of living.*

We have, as has been suggested, lost most of what was precious in these great philosophies. The idea of personal excellence has been pushed into the background to be replaced by the idea of duty. And the idea of virtue as a rare possession of the exemplary and thus superior person has given way to that of the equality of all persons, first of all in the eyes of God, and then, by custom and law. Thus the worst among us is declared to be as good as the best. This represents a very considerable change, one result of which is that modern readers can hardly study the great classical moralists with understanding. We read *into* the writings of these great philosophers our own ideas, many of which were quite foreign to their thinking. In doing so we miss a lot.

chapter 6

Socratic Ethics

Let us now examine more closely the thinking of the ancients on the basic ethical ideas that have been adumbrated. It is an examination that is certain to be fruitful, for we are now looking back at a civilization that probably excelled every other in its creative genius and certainly excelled every other, before or since, in philosophy. There is a great treasure there to be mined, and once you see what it is and come to appreciate its depth and originality, you can never again think about ethics in the ways you have been accustomed to.

GORGIAS, THE TEACHER OF RHETORIC

The conception of justice held by educated Athenians is beautifully illustrated in Plato's dialogue *Gorgias,* wherein Socrates is portrayed discussing that subject with three of his contemporaries. This dialogue perfectly expresses the conflict between the abstract and philosophical conceptions of justice embodied in Socrates' comments and the conventional conception taken for granted by virtually all educated Athenians of that day. It would not serve our purpose to undertake a summary of that brilliant and provocative dialogue as a whole, but it will serve perfectly to illustrate the original conception of justice held by the Greeks and thus lay the groundwork for much of what follows.

That original conception of justice is illustrated in Socrates' discussion with Gorgias himself, the first of the three partners engaged in discussion by Socrates. Gorgias was a teacher of rhetoric, whose instruction was much sought by the sons of the better families, young men aspiring to careers in politics or other positions of influence and leadership. He was something of a Dale Carnegie of antiquity. Dale Carnegie was a man who made himself wealthy in the earlier part of this century giving instruction in the techniques of winning friends and influencing people. Gorgias' aim was to instruct in the techniques of influence by the persuasive use of language, particularly in public discussion. His instruction was useful, too, to anyone accused of an offense and brought to trial. As there was no priesthood among the Athenians, so also there were no lawyers, and people had to plead their own cases. Skill in argument and debate, and in persuading others to one's point of view, was valuable. And Gorgias was just the person to train one in that art.

His conversation with Socrates involved a considerable amount of dialectical hair splitting, in which Socrates appears to be seeking nothing more significant than a good definition of the word *rhetoric*, but underlying this is a theme of considerable significance. Gorgias, aiming at precision, suggests that rhetoric has to do with producing belief by the use of words—a description that is, of course, far too broad inasmuch as it applies to any kind of oral instruction. The teacher of medicine uses words for that purpose, for example, yet he is not engaging in rhetoric. Ultimately Gorgias proposes that rhetoric is the art of persuasion with respect to matters of justice. What he means by this is fairly obvious and correct, namely, that those who debate matters of public policy and law in public assemblies or similar forums are engaged in rhetoric, that is, are trying to persuade by discussion and argument.

But, of course, this raises the deeper question concerning the nature of justice. Does the rhetorician know what it is? Do his students? Gorgias blithely answers that, of course, he knows what justice is, and so do his students; but in case any of them do not, he will instruct them in that, too.

This strikes the modern reader, as it did Socrates, as being either outrageously arrogant and presumptuous, or totally naive. Here is a man who is saying that he *knows* what justice is! He has a knowledge which even the gods, one would think, would hardly dare claim. And even worse, Gorgias is saying that the youths who come to him for instruction (men too young and callow to have yet begun to make their way in the world by themselves, mere boys still wet behind the ears, as we might say) understand justice! Now if that is not an outrageous and extravagant suggestion, then it is an unbelievably naive one; for it may be that Gorgias just does not realize what he is saying, that he is just being simple-minded.

In any case, Socrates has little difficulty making Gorgias look like a fool, and he does it by reading the strongest possible meaning into his claim. A person must, Socrates notes, be expert at that which he knows or undertakes to teach. By that token, then, one must in fact himself be *just* if he really knows justice—a claim that can hardly be made for Gorgias' pupils and one which Gorgias would hesitate to make for himself. Perfectly decent and well-intentioned these men may be, or for that matter may not be. In any case it cannot be claimed that they are without exception persons who exemplify justice in their lives—which is what Socrates claims we should expect, if they know what justice is.

Gorgias fails to see how he got tricked into this inference, but we can see if we look closely. And in doing so, we shall see what Gorgias meant by justice, and why he was in fact quite right in believing that the knowledge of it is perfectly common.

In thinking of justice, Gorgias did not have in mind any absolute and universal standard or even anything very profound. Gorgias was merely thinking of the customs and conventions of the Athenians in the more important matters of social intercourse and, particularly, in matters of commerce. He meant by justice the rules, written and unwritten, that people follow in living together and cooperating in common enterprises. It is when these are involved—when decisions must be made affecting public policy, for example, or when someone is summoned before judges to account for his actions—that rhetoric is needed. And of course any well-bred Athenian youth can be presumed to know justice in this sense, to know, in other words, the customs and laws of the Athenians. A claim to such knowledge is neither presumptuous nor naive but simply commonplace. Only a barbarian could fail to know what justice is, in this sense. In philosophical terms we can say that justice was, for Socrates' contemporaries, something purely conventional. It was Socrates, not Gorgias, who was arrogant and presumptuous, for it was Socrates who presumed that justice is something *other* than what it was clearly perceived to be by everyone else.

POLUS AND THE DOUBLE SENSE OF JUSTICE

This underlying conflict between a conventional and a natural sense of justice is also exhibited in Socrates' conversation with Polus who, in the Platonic dialogue under consideration, takes over from Gorgias. Polus declares what seems to him quite evident to any person with experience of the world, namely, that the perpetrator of an injustice is certainly not as bad off as the victim provided, of course, he escapes punishment. For example, one is clearly the loser if he is stolen from, and clearly the winner if he is the undetected thief. Similarly, it is the victim of an assault who suffers, not his assailant. So, in general, we can say that committing injustice is better than suffering it.

This seems self-evident. Why is it, then, that the commission of injustice is condemned, rather than the suffering of it? Because, Polus notes, the doing of injustice is uglier, more reprehensible, and somehow base.

Socrates, hearing this, must have realized that he would be able to make Polus look very foolish in a very few moves. For what Polus has just said is quite incoherent—that that which is ugly and base is nevertheless *better* than that which is not! Things that are base and ugly are bad; that is simply part of what it means to describe them in such terms. And things that are bad can hardly be better than things that are not. Polus is, in effect, saying that something that is ugly is fairer than something that is not, and something that is more evil is better than that which is less so. And these suggestions are quite inconsistent.

What is good and beautiful in its very nature, Socrates suggests, is justice. We need not even argue this; it is part of what the word means. So, whatever is characterized as just, such as a person, a law, an institution, or a practice is by that same fact characterized as beautiful and good.

Furthermore, people always seek what seems to them to be good. It is incomprehensible that any normal person would deliberately set about trying to get something that he believes would be bad for him. The point in calling something *good* is to recommend it, to say that it is worth seeking, and the point in describing something as *bad* is to say that it is not worth seeking or, indeed, that it should be shunned. Therefore when people, acting voluntarily, fail to achieve what is good in their actions, or when they miss the mark, this must be because they did not know what it was. They did not clearly see which goal was good and which bad. Failure of this kind is, in other words, due to ignorance. If one seeks what seems good (this being the invariable rule of voluntary action), and achieves only what is bad, then it follows that this person has failed to recognize the bad for what it was, mistaking it for something good.

THE SOCRATIC PARADOXES

Basing his arguments upon the foregoing suppositions, each of which is quite plausible when considered by itself, Socrates was able to deduce conclusions that seem wildly at odds with common sense, and get Polus to embrace those conclusions by the sheer logical force of his dialectic.

Thus, for example, Polus concedes that justice is something good, which seems incontestable. Accordingly, anything which is truly just must also be something good and, therefore, something preferred by anyone who sees what it is.

And from this it follows of course that anyone who has lapsed into injustice will, if he is intelligent and knows the real worth of things, seek punishment for himself—because such punishment will be just, hence good, hence something that anyone deserving it will certainly want to have! The intelligent criminal will be his own accuser; will seek out a prosecutor and judge and will rejoice when the deserved sentence is passed even though it may be a harsh and painful one.

The intelligent criminal is thus similar to those afflicted with disease who know that a cure exists. Such persons will seek a physician and gladly take the medicine, bitter as it may be, for they know that what they are getting is something good, however distasteful. The fool, on the other hand, will scorn the medicine, flee from the physician, and perhaps perish of the malady. Analogously, the wicked tyrant, thieves, or murderers who try to cover their tracks and prevent discovery of their acts from fear that they will be punished, are fools. And if they rejoice at their success in evading justice, then they are greater fools.

This is the kind of conclusion that Socrates was able to elicit from Polus, and it must be noted that his argument is perfectly valid, however absurd the conclusion may appear. If justice is good (as all admit), and hence all just things (such as deserved punishment) are also good (as seems to follow), and if all people in their voluntary actions seek things that are good when they are available (which seems to be a correct principle of voluntary action), then it does follow that a wicked person will, from self-interest, seek just punishment if he or she has any sense. The fact that the wicked usually do everything they can to evade such punishment, and often succeed, shows only how very stupid they are.

THE CROWNING PARADOX

But there is a stronger and even more paradoxical claim that can be made here, and Socrates does not neglect to press it. It can be expressed this way.

Let us suppose that you have been the victim of an enormous injustice. Suppose, for example, that some man has totally ruined you by deceit and fraud, destroyed your reputation by slander, and thereby enriched himself and gained positions of power and influence. We suppose, in short, that he is an immensely successful criminal, but at your expense. Out of your natural bitterness and resentment you have a keen, obsessive desire that he should suffer for his crimes. You want some great evil to befall him in repayment for the evil he has brought upon you.

Of course, the question can be raised whether anyone should ever wish evil upon anyone for whatever reason, but that is not the question to be considered here. Instead let us ask how, if it were within your power to make that person suffer, would you go about it? What is the greatest evil you could bring down upon him? Would it be to make him suffer pain for his crimes? To get him punished?

No, Socrates says, it would be the very opposite! Suppose you possess the incontestable proof of his criminality. We can imagine that you have documents that establish his guilt without doubt. You can give these documents to the prosecutor's office and be absolutely certain that your enemy will suffer severe punishment. Should you do it? No! Instead you should hide those documents, do everything you can to guard your enemy against suspicion, cover up for him, make sure that he does not get punished, that he spends the rest of his days exempt from any prosecution. Why? Because, as we have seen, justice is something beautiful and good, hence just punishment is something good too. So, if you bring just punishment down upon your foe, then you will be giving him something good and your purpose, we were supposing, is the opposite. The greatest evil you can hope to wish upon him is that he should *never* be punished because, by wallowing in his own wickedness and injustice, he already is deeply sunk in evil. If you really wish him to suffer, then leave him there, guard him from those who would punish him, and above all, see to it that justice to him never is done!

It is very important at this point to remember just what question is being considered. We are not asking how one should treat one's enemies. We are considering the purely hypothetical question of how one should go about bringing evil upon someone, in case that person deserves to suffer for his or her crimes. Socrates' answer turns out to be the very opposite of what would first occur to most persons. He says that *if* your purpose is to make someone suffer evil, then you should protect that person from punishment. And his point in saying this, and in eliciting agreement from Polus, is simply to expose the logical consequence of saying, as most persons do, that justice is something good and beautiful by its very nature.

THE CONCEPT OF POWER

The same point can be elicited through an analysis of the idea of *power*. What is power? Polus suggests that the most enviable of men is the powerful tyrant, answerable to no one, able to do anything he wants and commit any injustice without fear of punishment from anyone. But is he in fact powerful? Socrates suggests, paradoxically, that such a man has less actual power than the victims of his crimes, that he is in fact worse off than they are.

Now why? The underlying logic of Socrates' position is this: Power is the ability to get what one wants. To the extent that you can get whatever you want you have power, and to the extent that you cannot, you lack it. But what is it that people always want? They want good things, and they want to avoid the opposite. Power, accordingly, must be defined as the power to get good things. To the extent that people's actions produce for them only bad things, then to that extent they lack power. This is but a corollary of the same point. Justice, however, is what is acknowledged by all to be good and beautiful, and its opposite, injustice, always base and ugly. From which it does most certainly follow that the wicked tyrant, to the extent that his actions produce injustice, is *lacking* in power, not possessed of it—the precise opposite of what Polus, in keeping with common sense, has suggested.

Socrates' arguments with Polus are valid, and their premises are at least accepted by most people. Nearly everyone does declare, with Polus, that justice is good and the commission of injustice base and ugly, and that the suffering of it, though painful, is in no way reprehensible. If these statements are taken at face value, then one is logically driven to the extraordinary conclusions to which Socrates leads Polus. It is not to the point to say they are strange, paradoxical, and implausible. What is to the point is to note that they are supported by the views of justice and injustice that nearly everyone shares. Socrates treats these surprising inferences as philosophical discoveries, and if we do not accept them as such, it is obviously up to us to produce arguments as good as those of Socrates to show why we should not.

chapter 7

The Idea of Natural Law

The inferences Socrates extracts from Polus are sometimes referred to as the "Socratic paradoxes," and rightly so. They amount to asserting the very opposite of what everyone actually believes, and yet, paradoxically, they are derived from views of ethics and justice that nearly everyone shares. One can hardly avoid the suspicion of trickery and dishonesty on Socrates' part. Such suspicions are, however, certainly unfounded. There is nothing logically wrong with the arguments. Suspicion should be directed, instead, to the common-sense presuppositions from which those arguments are drawn, such as the belief in the inherent goodness of justice and the baseness of injustice.

THE SPEECH OF CALLICLES

This is the doubt that is raised by Callicles, the final participant in this extraordinary dialogue. Callicles claims that those presuppositions can each be understood in either of two senses, and that Socrates, in his arguments with both Gorgias and Polus, has simply exploited this ambiguity in order to confuse his opponents and extract from them ridiculous conclusions. Callicles thereby not only discloses the profundity of the problems that have been introduced, he also introduces us to one of the most important, and at the same time least appreciated, philosophical conceptions to be found anywhere in the literature of philosophy. Indeed, to understand Callicles is, in large measure, to understand ethics, not because he offers up a system that is faultless and complete, but because he challenges us to consider the origins of ethics and the possibility of a natural ethics that might actually contradict the things we have been taught by convention to believe in. Indeed, one can say that the whole battle between the ethical ideals of classical antiquity and those that eventually replaced them are encapsulated in the astonishing dialogue between Callicles and Socrates. Callicles here advances a theory of human nature, virtue, and justice that Socrates never actually refutes and one that has, in fact, never been refuted at all. It has, over the course of time, simply been superseded by another conception of ethics—one that is now quite generally taken for granted, but which Callicles utterly repudiated. Socrates does, indeed, appear to refute Callicles, but if you look closely at the discussion you will find that he does so only by subtly changing the subject.

Let us now get Callicles' theory before us as clearly and fully as we can.

NATURE VERSUS CONVENTION

There are, according to Callicles, two levels of justice, the *natural* and the *conventional*. By the natural principles of justice he means those which are in fact true, quite independently of any customs or conventions that human beings might adopt in this or that culture. Conventional justice, on the other hand, consists simply of the rules and customs that people adopt in order to enable them to get on with each other in a social life. These vary somewhat from one culture to another, unlike the natural principles that are the same everywhere, whether actually adhered to or not.

What is significant is that natural and conventional justice are often in serious conflict with each other. What is good by nature is sometimes deemed bad by human conventions. And this, according to Callicles, is exactly where Polus—and Gorgias too, for that matter—went wrong. They did not keep these two senses of justice distinct.

For example, when Gorgias said that he and his students know what justice is, he was, according to Callicles, obviously talking about conventional justice. He was only making the obvious and uncontroversial point that he and his students are familiar with the customs and conventions of the Athenians. But Socrates then took him to mean justice, in the *natural* sense, that is, to be claiming to know the true and absolute principles of justice that are valid everywhere. The two disputants were, in fact, talking about two different things.

So also for Polus. When he said it is uglier or more reprehensible to commit injustice than to suffer it, he was only speaking from the standpoint of convention. From the standpoint of nature, Callicles says, there is nothing wrong with doing what is unjust by conventional standards.

And what is this natural justice to which Callicles is appealing? It is the rule of the superior, of the true and natural aristocracy. This, he says, is what would prevail if natural principles were not being continually infected with the false values of convention.

We can see the force of Callicles' philosophy if we consider again the Greek conception of virtue that underlies it. Virtue meant for the Greeks, and for Callicles, personal excellence. It did *not* mean for them, as it usually does for us, adherence to conventional norms. On the contrary, it was—for Callicles at least—incompatible with that sense of virtue; and it was precisely, he thought, because Socrates kept shifting back and forth between these two senses that he was able to produce his absurd inferences.

Some of the virtues are natural endowments of those who have them. Intelligence is a good example. Natural intelligence, in case one is lucky enough to have it to a high degree, can of course be corrupted by conditions of life, such as severe deprivation; but no social or environmental conditions can create it. Other examples of natural virtues are physical beauty, strength, creative power, sensitivity to things subtle and beautiful, resourcefulness, and so on. Of course no persons are born with these virtues, but some are born with the capacity for them, and some rare individuals have, by nature, the capacity for the development of some of them to a very high degree. These are the truly exemplary people, the ones who stand out as naturally better than the hordes of people who lack these great gifts. These, in short, are the people (few in number) who are truly virtuous in the classical Greek sense.

It is important here to resist any temptation to object that persons are hardly worthy of praise for those capacities which were merely thrust on them by nature, such as intelligence or strength, and about which they had no choice. This is precisely to confuse *our* idea of virtue with the Greek idea. Virtue, for them, had no necessary connection with choice or will. That is an essentially Christian idea, which we have inherited; but it was quite foreign to the thinkers of Callicles' time. What needs to be remembered is that virtue, for them, had primarily to do with what one *is,* not what one *does.* Callicles, for example—and Aristotle, too, for that matter—would have difficulty thinking of any person who is physically weak or of slight stature as being in any significant sense good or noble. Nor would they understand the comment, so natural to someone of our culture, that people can hardly be thought "responsible" for their size! What, they would wonder, has that to do with virtue? And, given their conception of virtue, they would be entirely correct.

If the virtues are rare, and the combination of many of them in a single person rare indeed, then it did seem obvious to Callicles that the world and politics should be ordered for their sake and for their advantage. This did not mean that superior persons should be allowed to enrich themselves at the expense of others less noble; for that again is a purely modern and narrow conception of "advantage." It means, simply, that the noble, the natural aristocracy, should occupy their natural and rightful place in society, which is at the top. They should rule, for their own sakes, simply because they are the good.

THE ORIGIN OF CONVENTIONAL ETHICS

Since that is the dictate of nature, why is it so at odds with conventional morality? Callicles' philosophy provides an answer that is so convincing, so apparently grounded in correct understanding of human nature, that it seems never to have been refuted, by Socrates or anyone else.

The masses of people, Callicles says, are weak. By this he means simply that they do not possess, in any great degree, those natural gifts of intelligence, resourcefulness, courage, and the like, that make others stand out as better. By and large, most people are rather ignorant, stupid, insensitive—in a word "weak"—that is, inferior. This relative inferiority of the many evokes in them a justified feeling of their inferiority together with a concern for their own well-being. They fear that they will be taken advantage of by those who are better. And in this, too, they are right. According to Callicles, the good and noble, always relatively few in number, will *and should* govern for the advancement of their own interests, not for the limited and frivolous interests of the masses.

So the weak, perceiving this, invent restraints upon the superior in the form of moral rules. The very first principle of this morality is that *all people are equal*—something that is patently false but which, nevertheless, enables the many weak to *feel* that they are just as good as the truly virtuous! This false claim also protects them from exploitation by making it "unjust." That the superior should fare better than the inferior is perhaps not unfair; but if . all persons are declared to be equal, then the worst among us is raised to the same status as the best, and no one can properly take advantage of anyone.

And thus, according to Callicles, arises conventional justice. What is important in Callicles' claim is that this man-made justice, which we are all taught to believe in, is opposed to natural or true justice and is really, therefore, *injustice*. And this, once one sees its significance, is a very alarming possibility indeed. Callicles, in effect, invites us to consider it possible—in fact he is convinced that it is true—that the conventional principles of justice that we are taught from childhood to honor are in fact wrong, unjust, and sources of corruption; instead of making us better they make us worse, rendering it impossible for any true principles of justice to prevail. It is as if, in the name of truth and beauty, we were taught to honor error and ugliness. It is to "turn everything upside down," which is precisely what Callicles accuses Socrates of doing.

THE CONCEPT OF VIRTUE

Given his basic conception of what human virtue is—and it was a conception generally shared by the Greeks—Callicles' moral philosophy has to be basically correct. If you want to understand the ethical ideals of the Greeks, do not think of virtue as having to do with what a person *does*. Think of it, instead, as having to do with what one *is*. Everything has its unique excellence or virtue. One could hardly expect a human being to be an exception to this. Ask what the unique excellence of a person is—not this or that person but just a person as such. When you have the answer to that, you will know what it is that makes one person better than another and what makes some few stand out as truly noble or excellent.

One might take issue with Callicles with respect to what the distinctively human qualities are. He summed them up as "strength," and evidently had in mind the kind of intelligence, resourcefulness, courage, vision, and creative power that has always distinguished persons of greatness. Or one might, while accepting such qualities as genuine virtues, quarrel with Callicles' supposition that persons possessed of them should rule in their own interest. Really, all that Callicles was assuming here was that the better should prevail over the worse, which is plausible enough. He even thought it was a natural principle, obvious to anyone who thinks about it. Most people, on the other hand, hold that the nobler among us are entitled to no more than the least: that everyone should be treated the same—the very opposite of what Callicles declares. But he, it will be recalled, had a very good explanation for why most people feel that way. It is precisely because they are, in truth, inferior with respect to the virtues he has in mind that they declare all persons to be equal. That, then, is a man-made principle or a law of convention whereas Callicles' principle purports to come from nature. Here, once again, the conventional morality, which most people take for granted as obvious, is a perversion of the true principle and thus the expression of a corrupt morality. The fact that this corrupt morality is so widely adhered to does not show that it is true but only that most people would like to treat it as if it were true.

THE IDEAL OF REASON

Socrates' great contribution to philosophy and to western culture was his extolling of reason as the distinctive human quality and the focal point of human virtue. He was not, of course, the first to use reason nor the first to praise it. On the contrary, Greek philosophy was, from its beginnings, uncompromisingly rational. One does not find anywhere in Greek philosophy an appeal to divination or the supernatural. More important, the Greeks were the first to cultivate philosophy as we know it, that is, as the search for truth for its own sake, using experience and reason as their sole guides. But Socrates was the first thinker of significant stature to try basing *ethics* upon reason and to try uncovering its natural principles solely by the use of reason. In this, it should be noted, he was in agreement with Callicles. Both thought there are true and natural principles of ethics. Both saw clearly the difference between natural principles and conventional ones. They differed only with respect to what those principles are. Socrates took it to be a natural principle of justice that no one, of whatever stature, should have an undue share of anything, whereas Callicles thought that the basic natural principle of justice implied the opposite.

The primary ethical value that survived this most critical period of Greek thought, the Socratic or Sophistic period, was rationality. It was not always clear what the ancients meant by reason, just as it is often not clear what modern thinkers mean by it. Some, following Socrates, identified it with the governing "part" of the soul. Others identified it with nature, that is, with certain changeless truths. Others considered it to be the same thing as philosophy, understood as the disinterested quest for knowledge and wisdom. The ancients did not contrast it with religious faith, for that was an idea foreign to the pre-Christian era. That contrast, however, eventually came into being, and the ground was prepared for the long cultural war which followed and which is still being fought. No two values would seem to offer less hope of reconciliation with each other than faith and reason, since the claims of one seem to be the absolute repudiation of the other.

We cannot enter upon a history of that long struggle. What is important for our purposes is that out of it emerged modern and contemporary philosophical ethics. The ethics of Christianity had no need for reason, whose voice it considered weak indeed compared with the voice of God disclosed in Scripture. Philosophy, on the other hand, by its very nature had no use for sacred texts, being already in possession of the profoundest and noblest writings ever to flow from unaided human reason. The groundwork was laid for some great philosopher, someday, to convince the world that the two paths lead to the same result and that the expressions of God's will for his creatures correspond with what the unaided human reason can also discover. We have yet to consider whether that reassuring claim can be successfully defended.

chapter 8

Cynics and Stoics

Socrates' moral philosophy, though often expressed in highly paradoxical claims, was essentially very conservative. He simply assumed that the principles of justice and morality that the Athenians honored were true principles, or, in other words, natural ones. There was thus little possibility of any basic conflict between nature and convention in his thinking.

The immediate effect of his thinking on his spiritual descendants was, however, quite revolutionary. What the Sophists had done was call attention to the conventional character of Athenian ideas of justice, and certainly Socrates never cast doubt upon the idea that there are also natural principles of justice. Picking this up, his successors made it their first order of business to repudiate convention in the name of something nobler and in the fullest sense true, namely, nature. Thus arose the enduring ideal, "Live according to nature." That ideal is still with us and is the veritable mother's milk of philosophy, although we have substituted the word *reason* for *nature,* with virtually no change at all in the original meaning of the exhortation.

CYNICISM

The initial, profound effect of Socratic and Sophistic teaching is abundantly evident in the Cynic school. The Cynics took their name from the

Kynosarges, a gymnasium in Athens where Antisthenes, their founder, offered instruction in moral philosophy. The name Cynic happened, however, to be the same as the Greek word for "doglike," which reinforced the impression among the Athenians that these people repudiated the basic rules of civilized life.

The Cynics were convinced of the purely conventional foundation of Athenian values and customs, which meant to them that they had no rational foundation at all. It was, therefore, their primary aim to reject those customs and values in favor of what is correct and worthwhile by nature. We should live, they declared, not according to the false values that human beings have fabricated but according to nature.

It was a shallow philosophy, with little theoretical foundation other than the inspiration of Socrates, but the Cynics made a valuable point and drove it home dramatically by their behavior. Diogenes, their most famous representative, stands out as the devastating critic and exposer of peoples' pretentiousness and arrogance. Dedicated to poverty—since wealth is a purely human or conventional value and hence of no worth—Diogenes got the necessities of life from begging, concentrating his energies upon the perfection of himself as a person. He did this with such ingenuousness, humor, and self-ridicule as to endear himself to everyone forever. Once, for example, found begging before a statue, he explained that he was practicing fortitude in being refused! He lived in a tub, scorning all possessions except the few necessities that could be carried in a purse. Having at one time owned a drinking cup, he cast this aside as a superfluous, and hence worthless, encumbrance when he saw a mouse drinking from a puddle. Even Alexander the Great did not awe him, for Diogenes saw him only as another human being like himself but heaped up with conventional, and hence worthless, tokens and values. Alexander, awesome on his white horse, appeared one day before Diogenes, who was sunning himself in front of his tub, and announced that he was Alexander, "the great king." To which Diogenes replied that he was Diogenes, the dog. "Do you not fear me?" asked Alexander. To this Diogenes responded, "Are you good or evil?" "Good, of course!" said the other. And Diogenes asked, "How could anyone be so foolish as to fear what is good?" The king was so struck by this that he offered the Cynic anything he wanted—to which Diogenes replied, "Then please stand out of my sunlight!"

Here, again, is the Socratic type of play on the word "good," to mean *either* superior in the qualities characteristic of a noble person, *or* to mean fair, just, and reasonable. The former might indeed be an object of fear to someone as meek and helpless as Diogenes, but clearly not the latter. We have also the cynical contempt for purely human values, such as the status of kingship (no better than that of a dog), as well as for the conventional gifts that a king might deliver (of less worth than the sunlight, which is a gift of nature).

THE STOICS

It was left to the Stoics to forge a clear, profound, and heroic morality upon the ideal of a perfectly rational life. As the Cynics flamboyantly scorned convention in their dedication to nature, so the Stoics scorned human feeling. Their slogan was the same—"Live according to nature"; but to them this meant an uncompromising subordination of all their desires and feelings to what is by nature unavoidably true. Nature, for the Greeks, meant not only what is true, independently of human fabrication, but also what is unalterable. Indeed, the two ideas seemed to them necessarily connected. Whatever is made true by human action is a conventional truth, but nature is composed of that vast realm of fact which can be neither made nor undone by any human act. If there are truths of justice in that realm, then we had better adjust our conventional justice to them as Callicles had insisted. And in any case, as the Stoics always claimed, wisdom will consist in not resisting nature, or in trying to avoid the unavoidable, or in altering what exists by necessity.

The Stoic philosophy, like most moral philosophy of the ancients, was a quest for personal excellence or perfection, not an attempt to ferret out any ultimate principles of moral right and wrong. In keeping with what was generally assumed in their culture, they thought obligations are determined by role or function. A king has a function; so does a parent; so likewise a soldier, and so on. One's duty, then, is very straightforward and obvious: Perform your role or function well. If you are a father, your duty is to be a good one, and that is something within your power. It is not your duty to ensure that your children grow up to be good people, because that is for them to determine. This is not within your power, but theirs.

You search in vain in the Stoic writings for guides to moral conduct, as we understand morality. The guides that are offered are simply to rational conduct and, more important, rational attitudes. Personal excellence or perfection, that is to say a totally rational life, is one and the same with happiness, and one and the same with virtue. Do you wish to attain the greatest blessing available to mortals? Then find it within yourself in the perfection of your own inner nature, which is your rationality. Having found it, you will have found the only genuine goodness there is. And that will surely be the *eudaemonia* that every moralist has been seeking; indeed, what else could it possibly be? And what, moreover, can the perfection of your nature be other than the perfection of reason, since that is precisely what your nature is? The rational principle is the governing principle. It is by your reason that you know what is true, that you understand nature, and it is by the same reason that you are able to adjust your thought and feeling to what you thus know. Your feelings, accordingly, must always be subordinated to this reason exactly as Socrates taught. Feelings are shared with animals, and while they may impel us this way and that, blindly, they guide us to nothing whatever. Do not try to make nature agreeable to your feelings, but adjust your feelings to nature and live accordingly.

The Stoic philosophy is inspired, and cold. The Stoic philosopher impresses us as an unfeeling statue who is, by the same token, incorruptible. There is no evil, he says, except in the view you take of things. Nothing that happens can possibly affect *you* adversely; for, again as Socrates had taught, the only evil that can befall a rational person is the corruption of his nature (that is, of his reason) and this is the one thing in the world that is always within our control. The tyrant can imprison my body, but he cannot touch my inner self or my reason. So let him do as he will with my body; it is nothing to *me*. The tyrant can frighten me only if I choose to let my feelings, rather than my will, govern my reason. If I think something will harm me, then I am already harmed by my foolish fear; but if I know that nothing outside of myself can harm me, then I am already invincible.

Once you grasp the basic principle of the Stoic philosophy, which is dedication to virtue conceived as personal excellence, then you are able to see the rigor and consistency with which the Stoic applied it to daily life. Unlike the Cynics, for example, the Stoics did not carry their indifference to conventional goods to outright scorn and rejection of them. They only insisted that such goods not be objects of *desire,* since desire is something opposed to reason. Epictetus, the Roman Stoic and exemplar of this ancient ideal, illustrated this by comparing the behavior of a rational adult with that of a child. If figs and nuts are thrown into the air where children are playing, he noted, the children, instantly succumbing to desire, scramble for them, fighting and yelling in response to their greed. A rational being does not do this, even though what is dangled before him might be a much greater temptation—powerful position, wealth, great honor, or the other alluring things with which the world entices us. Let the children among us scramble for these, Epictetus says; the Stoic will retain his calm and rational reserve. But then he asks, "What if a fig or nut drops right into your lap?" Discard it? No, take it, for a fig or nut is worth just so much.

You can see the point of that anecdote if you imagine yourself to be one of many possible heirs to the fortune of some rich uncle. Let the others flatter him and try to ingratiate themselves with him in the hope of favor and fortune. You, following the Stoic principle, will remain yourself, aloof from this grasping and greed, doing what is appropriate to your role, and indifferent to the outcome. But what if you find yourself the inheritor of this estate? Accept it; it is worth just so much. What it is *not* worth is compromising your integrity to get it, because integrity is the governing principle of your life.

DUTY AND THE TREATMENT OF OTHERS

What, then, of our treatment of others? Love and affection are not rational. They are expressions of feeling. Should they too be scorned along with the feelings that are corrupting?

"Yes," the Stoic says; but this will not mean scorning the persons to whom such love and affection might otherwise be directed. Any appropriate actions to which love might prompt one, reason can prompt one more reliably.

Suppose, for example, you come upon a distraught man, groaning and weeping over his misfortunes. His son has fallen into bad ways, and is leading a worthless life, demolishing all the high hopes his family had for him. What, if you are a Stoic, do you do? You first remind yourself that no evil has befallen this man. It is only in the view he takes of things. The only bad thing that could happen to him would be for something to make *him* worse. No fate of his son can have that result. One suffers evil, or is made worse, only if one's own personal excellence or goodness, that is the capacity to live according to reason or nature, is corrupted, as Socrates has shown. Nothing like this has happened to this disconsolate man.

Does the Stoic then pass him by with indifference? *No,* for one has a duty, even to this stranger, to console him in his misery. So you sit down with him and even, as Epictetus says, groan with him if necessary—being careful, however, not to groan inwardly too!

What is the meaning of that? It is a perfect expression of the idea that duty, rather than love, is the proper and rational motive in our dealings with others. You *act* as you would act if you loved, but you resolutely suppress any inclination to love, for that is a mere feeling and hence irrational.

The compelling force for the Stoic in such a situation is not one's obligations *to others,* much less any love for them, but rather, one's obligation *to oneself.* That obligation is, as always, to tend and reinforce one's own excellence as a person (or what the ancients called virtue). You help the suffering, not for their sake, but because to do otherwise would be to compromise the sense of obligation that is essential to a truly noble life.

So, to this picture of stopping to assist the suffering we can add the following reflection: If your succor were to no avail, even if the person you were trying to help were made worse by your efforts, still that would be no reason to reproach yourself or to regret anything. For you were not trying to do something for the other person except incidentally. Instead, you were trying to fulfill your proper role as a rational human being. And in that you have succeeded no matter what the outcome of your efforts so far as others are concerned.

One can hardly help contrasting this picture, from Epictetus, with the strikingly similar one, from the Gospels, concerning the Samaritan. The contrast is enormous when it is realized that Jesus gave the story of the

Samaritan precisely to illustrate what it means to love a neighbor, even a despised one!

"I met Epictetus," someone once declared, "and it was like meeting a statue." A statue is loveless and cold. But it is also not subject to desire or corruption. What lay behind the statue-like exterior of Epictetus was the clearest imaginable conception of virtue. A person's virtue, or strength, or excellence—these words all mean the same thing here—is the perfection of what is unique in him as a person, achieved only by the cultivation of his proper or distinguishing function. And that function, of course, is reason. We have always before us, then, the choice between reason, which is nobility, and desire and its objects, which is baseness. These objects of desire, however brilliantly they may shine and however tempting they may be to our wills, are in themselves of no value; but they are corrupting to reason.

THE IMPACT OF THE STOIC IDEAL OF REASON

These Stoic themes, soon overwhelmed by the Christian ethical ideas that were making their appearance at about that time, eventually surfaced again in the moral philosophy of Immanuel Kant, particularly the emphasis upon reason rather than feeling as the basis of ethics.

We shall turn to that immensely important development at the appropriate place, but here we can note the confluence of ideas that gave Kantian ethics its importance. On the one side is the idea of virtue, which ancient pagan philosophy identified with personal excellence, that is, with what one *is*. On the other side was a different idea of virtue, identified by the Christians with obedience to God's laws, that is, with what one *does*. Kant united these two very different ideas of virtue into the concept of a law that is founded not on faith but upon reason. Thereby, in one stroke, he united the seemingly irreconcilable philosophical and religious ethical traditions, appearing to preserve what was precious in both. It is probably no exaggeration to say that no one can understand modern philosophical ethics, and Kant's role in its development, who does not appreciate the point that was just made.

chapter 9

Platonism and Ethical Relativism

The ethical thinking of the ancient pagan moralists tended, as we have seen, to go in two diametrically opposed directions. On the one hand, we find the tendency towards rationalism and ethical absolutism embodied in the thinking of Socrates and his philosophical descendants, most notably the Stoics. On the other side, we find the pragmatic and empirical emphasis characteristic of Gorgias and the Sophists generally. The first of these tendencies is perfectly illustrated by Plato's philosophy and the other by the views associated with Protagoras, the archetypal Sophist.

PLATONIC ABSOLUTISM

Socrates tended to treat all nouns as referring to real things. Indeed, this has been more or less characteristic of philosophers ever since. Thus, words like *river, mountain,* and *tree* derive their meaningfulness from the fact that they refer to certain things—namely, to rivers, to mountains, and to trees. What, then, of such words as *justice, pleasure,* and *goodness*? These too are nouns, and they are meaningful. It is easy to suppose that they, too, must refer to real things—namely, to justice, to pleasure, and to goodness. And then the philosopher's task becomes that of achieving a better understanding of those things to which such words are thought to refer, there being no doubt that they must be real, even though quite intangible.

Plato carried this to such an extreme that the very word, *Platonism*, has come to refer to that tendency, even in areas of thought having nothing to do with Plato's actual writings. Thus Plato spoke of goodness—or, as he preferred to call it, "the good"—as though it were a real being, more real, indeed, than the visible, earthly things which he sometimes described as imperfectly "partaking" of it. Though not visible, he thought it could be apprehended by intelligence, that is, by the rational faculty. In fact, Plato thought it was the ultimate goal of reason to attain to just this apprehension. And it was this very capacity of philosophy to *know* the good that justified philosophers in claiming the title of kings in an ideal state.

This is no place for an excursion into Platonic metaphysics, but the effect upon ethics of the mode of thought just described should be fairly obvious. That effect has been to treat all the usual ethical distinctions as natural ones, not conventional ones. Justice, for example, in Plato's philosophy, is not seen as consisting simply of customary practices, originated by human beings in order to facilitate social life, and variable from one time or place to another. The possibility is not even entertained that justice could ever be something other than what it is. Instead, the distinction between justice and injustice is seen as being as natural as the distinction between health and sickness—with which, in fact, Plato sometimes compared it.

Henceforth, then, under Plato's influence, the tendency among philosophers will be to look at human institutions and laws as always imperfect, always needing correction so as to approximate more nearly the perfect goodness and justice evisaged by reason. The principles of justice, no longer thought of as customary, will be represented as constituting a great *natural* law, as invariant as the heavens and as awesome. Eventually, of course, this natural law of the philosophers will be combined with to the divine law to which believers bow. Then, as faith declines, but the religious conception of morality persists, this same natural law, now having acquired the form of a command, will find its way back to philosophy and be represented, once more, as the discovery of reason. Kant, in fact, will proclaim the duty expressed in this great command to be as awesome as the starry heavens; and, while it will not be represented as emanating from there, as the expression of God's will, its authority will not be greatly diminished because the authority of reason will have replaced the waning authority of faith.

PLATO'S REPUBLIC

What we know of Socrates is almost entirely gleaned from Plato's dialogues, so it is not always possible to be sure whether the philosophy expressed in some of those dialogues is that of Socrates or of Plato. It does not matter much so far as we are concerned, for Plato's moral philosophy, like Stoicism, is certainly based squarely upon Socratic presuppositions.

The Republic, however, does incontestably express Plato's philosophy. It is a puzzling book, but one sees its richness only when it is placed in the context of the three ideas that dominated moral philosophy of that age, the ideas of virtue or excellence, happiness, and justice. *The Republic* is represented by its author as a discussion of justice, and yet we search in vain for some of the themes that a modern reader associates with this concept. Hardly anything is said, for example, about the rights of citizens, the manner in which trials are to be conducted, the treatment of slaves, or the conduct of relations with other states. Even the idea of fairness, which seems to us inseparable from justice, is hardly found there at all. And needless to say, the ideas of moral right and wrong as we understand them have no significant role in this classical discourse on justice.

Justice, it turns out, is simply virtue or personal excellence all over again, conceived, as by Socrates, as the cultivation of reason. A just person, according to Plato, is one whose reason governs his appetites and will. Injustice is the usurpation of reason's role by desire. And in the state, similarly, justice will consist of rule by a small and elite group, the paragons of the rational life, namely, the philosophers.

And what of the third idea, happiness? How is it attained, either by an individual or a state? Plato's answer is that a genuinely happy individual *is* the individual he has described, the one who embodies justice in his soul and in his life. Similarly, the happy commonwealth is the very state Plato imaginatively describes. Happiness, then, is not a reward of justice and virtue. The three things are inseparably connected. One achieves justice by the perfection of human excellence. And human excellence is, once again, the cultivation of reason. And having attained a fully rational life, one has thereby also attained the good life, which is precisely what the Greeks identified with happiness.

In effect, Plato advises that one not look to someone's words and deeds to see whether that person is just. That will tell you only whether he or she speaks and acts in the manner prescribed by the conventional norms of justice. Seek out, instead, the qualities of the soul; in other words, ascertain the nature of the inner person. Is it harmonious? That is, are the will and desires properly subordinated to the governance of reason? And is the rational faculty perfected to the point that this person knows—as distinct from merely believing—what the abiding principles of goodness are? If so, you are confronted with someone who is not only the embodiment of justice but of virtue and happiness as well. Let this rational being—who knows what is true, and who is in perfectly rational control of desire—be in control of society, and you will find the same three attributes of justice, virtue, and happiness embodied there. In short, let kings be philosophers, and let philosophers be kings; and the very excellence that moralists seek in the lives of individuals will also be found in the state.

Unless a modern reader studies *The Republic* against the idea of human excellence that was the theme of virtually all Greek moral philosophy, it will remain essentially a closed book. If we begin our reading of that book thinking of justice as something connected with morality in the modern sense—that is, as having to do with what is dutiful and right—then we shall simply miss the point. Greek moral philosophy was not primarily concerned with right and wrong. The moralists, for the most part, assumed that these distinctions were quite familiar to civilized people and not of primary philosophical importance. Their philosophical approach to ethics was that of aspiration, not duty. What was important to them was the correct ideal of human nature and, for Plato, the correct ideal of a *polis*. This ideal was to be found and attained, they thought, not through the drawing of distinctions between right and wrong, but rather through the understanding of a human being's true function or purpose, which was quite generally assumed by them to be the cultivation of reason. The ideal state like the ideal person will be one governed by perfected reason. It is in that direction that virtue surely lies and with it justice and happiness as well. But we do have to remember the uniquely Greek meanings that were attached to the ideas of justice and happiness and not try reading into them our own associations with those terms. Otherwise, how shall we ever understand them? And without understanding them, how shall we ever be able to decide which approach to ethics is to be perfected, theirs or ours?

THE CONVENTIONALISM OF PROTAGORAS

Socrates, and all his philosophical descendants, took for granted that the basic distinctions of ethics are grounded in nature just as surely as are the basic distinctions of medicine or mathematics. Neither the physician nor anyone else creates the distinction between health and disease, nor could all of the mathematicians of the world alter the difference between the odd and the even. These distinctions are just given, to be understood by reason and sometimes used in the pursuit of a rational life, but never to be abolished or altered in any way.

There was, however, another school of thought on this, and it is perfectly represented by Socrates' contemporary Protagoras. This great man's thought has been eclipsed by his now more famous rival, but it is significant that, in his own day, his intellectual stature appears to have exceeded that of Socrates and indeed everyone else. Today he is usually thought of, disparagingly, as the paradigmatic Sophist, but that is largely because our image of him has been thoroughly colored by Plato's jaundiced view of all the Sophists, whom he dismissed as dishonest dealers in spiritual wares.

Protagoras understood perfectly the distinction between nature and convention, and the similar distinction between knowledge and opinion, as did Socrates and Plato. Nature, it will be recalled, encompasses all the things that are given as true, independently of human intervention, and which are thus unalterably true. And it is these truths that are the objects of knowledge. Convention, on the other hand, encompasses those things that are true only because some person or persons have made them true. These are the unstable truths embodied in opinion. What distinguishes Protagoras from his Socratic rivals is that, as they tended to ascribe everything to nature, in the sense just defined, he tried to ascribe everything to convention. Nothing, he said, is true by nature, and so there is no actual knowledge of anything. All truth is conventional, and we must forever be content with opinion, that is, with beliefs that are neither true nor false in any final sense and which are subject to constant modification. "Man," he said, "is the measure of *all* things." Hence, not only are the principles of justice and virtue of purely human origin, varying from one time and place to another, so are all the principles underlying the whole of human wisdom. We should not speak of *knowledge* of anything but only of opinion, and opinions, of course, can differ. No opinion is really true nor is any really false—though some opinions, as Protagoras conceded, are *better* than others. Opinions are *good* ones in case they enable one to get on well and achieve things. And they are *bad* ones in case they lead to defeat and frustration. In neither case are they true or false. Thus any ordinary citizen who believed himself to be king, or any invalid who believed himself to be as strong as the wrestlers, would soon learn the folly of such notions. This would also apply to political states. Their laws, practices, and institutions cannot be meaningfully described as just or unjust, there being no actual standard against which to measure them. But the laws, practices, and institutions of states are in some cases better and in some cases worse than others, meaning by this that they work either well or ill in terms of the happiness and well-being of those who live under them.

What, then, of virtue? The Socratic school thought of virtue as the fulfillment of one's natural function, which, without exception, they took to be the exercise of reason. The good life was for them, accordingly, the fully rational life. Protagoras' conception of virtue was less metaphysical, much more in keeping with experience; and it is on this part of his philosophy that his fame rested.

Protagoras thought of virtue as consisting simply of those traits of character that are prized and nourished by a given culture. The intellectual life is indeed virtue for cultivated Athenians; but that is not the virtue of the Spartans, the Egyptians, or the Ethiopians. And there are, of course, other virtues even for Athenians, for example, courage and temperance. To call them virtues is to say no more than that they are regarded as such within a given culture. A virtuous person is no more than one who fulfills the ideals of character that have been imparted to him by those around him. Within another culture other norms are apt to prevail, and there is no point in asking which ones express the correct ideal of virtue. Each is as correct as any other; for there is, by nature, no distinction between what is and what is not correct in this realm nor, indeed, in any other.

When Socrates asked Protagoras (in Plato's dialogue of that name) whether he thought virtue could be taught, and if so, who the teachers would be, Protagoras had no trouble in answering. He said that of course it can be taught, since it in fact *is*, and that everyone is the teacher of it. What he meant by this, of course, is that young people, in the process of growing up, absorb the customs and ideals of their culture. And this is all that is meant by saying that they learn virtue, and that, accordingly, virtue is taught. But no special teachers are needed for this any more than special teachers are needed to learn one's native tongue. Virtue, like language, is simply imbibed.

"VULGAR" VERSUS "INTELLECTUAL" VIRTUE

Of course one can hardly fail to note that Protagoras is obviously right in this, given his conception of virtue as consisting essentially of customary habits of thought and conduct. We do learn these in precisely the way Protagoras says, and our teachers are simply those around us who significantly influence our character development.

What is still at issue, however, is whether the conventionalism upon which Protagoras rests his moral philosophy is or is not the real foundation of ethics. If we are talking about the distinction between moral right and wrong, then Protagoras is doubtless right. That distinction is created by moral rules, and it is hard to see what source those rules could have other than human conventions. They seem to be nothing but the customs and laws governing conduct that this or that culture adopts over the course of time. This was sometimes referred to by the ancients as "vulgar" virtue or, in other words, the virtue of common people.

If, on the other hand, one thinks of virtue in terms of personal excellence or, in other words, in terms of those strengths of character that set some individuals apart as superior to or better than others of their own culture, then Protagoras' moral philosophy is far less plausible than Plato's. For it still remains a possibility that, contrary to Protagoras, some human strengths are natural and their cultivation, therefore, better by nature. And, indeed, intelligence or the capacity for a rational life does seem to be precisely that natural strength that sets us apart from all other creatures. If so, the perfection of that capacity is, as the Socratics never doubted, exactly what sets one person apart from others as a truly better person. Protagoras has shown us an alternative to this way of looking at ethics, but he has offered no convincing reason for embracing that alternative. What he has done, instead, is to mix together (as if they were the same thing) the "vulgar virtue" of the masses, which consists simply of adherence to custom, and the "intellectual virtue" of the philosophers, which consists of a kind of personal excellence that can never be the possession of more than the few who are, indeed, better.

It remained for Aristotle to incorporate both conceptions of virtue into his philosophical ethics. Conventional virtue was not dismissed by Aristotle as worthless as it had in effect been by the Socratic schools. At the same time, it was not treated as the sum and substance of virtue, as it had been by Protagoras. Instead, Aristotle distinguished two levels of virtue, one of them conventional and the other rational or, as he called it, "intellectual." His moral philosophy thus represents a culmination of the two distinct traditions of Greek ethical thought. It cannot be understood apart from those traditions, which were outlined earlier, any more than contemporary philosophical ethics can be understood independently of the Greek and Christian traditions, as we shall soon discover.

chapter 10

Aristotle's Ethics

Aristotle's *Nicomachean Ethics* is probably the most widely read treatise on moral philosophy ever written. It avoids, for the most part, extreme positions and is composed in the careful, analytical style that immensely appeals to academic moralists, particularly in the English-speaking world.

That great work is probably also the most widely misunderstood treatise on this subject precisely because modern interpreters read into it their own ideas of ethics and neglect to place Aristotle's thought within the context of his own culture and, in particular, within the context of the idea of personal excellence, or nobility, that Aristotle so perfectly expresses.

For example, modern readers tend to treat Aristotle's famous description of the proud man as a curiosity, as something out of place in his scheme of ethics, even as an embarrassment. In truth, however, that description of pride is perhaps the most characteristically Aristotelian passage in the entire book. It expresses what Aristotle thought philosophical ethics should be concerned with. It perfectly expresses the ethics of aspiration, or the search for the truly ideal human being. The fact that modern moralists take such a low view of pride, or of the superiority of some people over others, is the result of an acculturation, religious in origin, that was entirely foreign to Aristotle.

Again, Aristotle's extensive application of the principle of moderation is sometimes understood by modern readers to constitute his analysis of the distinction between right and wrong conduct. There are actually students of this work who simply assume that what Aristotle is saying, essentially, is that actions are right if they fit a pattern of the mean, and wrong if they fall short of or exceed it! And that is to reduce Aristotle's ethics to utter triviality.

Aristotle says virtually nothing in the entire book about right and wrong. This should astonish those who assume (as most people do but as Aristotle did not) that the concepts of right and wrong are at the very center of any discussion of ethics. In fact, it is doubtful whether Aristotle even had any conception of what we refer to as *moral* right and wrong. His references to right and wrong are incidental, and not parts of his main themes. When, for example, he notes that friends will not wrong each other, he is mainly making a point about what is base or shameful in the light of an ideal. He is not calling attention to any supposed philosophical distinction between moral right and wrong. And his extensive discussion of the principle of moderation is intended as an analysis of *the virtues*, not of any presumed distinction between right and wrong. Furthermore, the virtues there under consideration are essentially conventional ones. His appeal is, constantly, to the character of the conventionally correct and civilized Athenian. Thus, from the very start, Aristotle is concerned with human excellence.

THE TWO KINDS OF VIRTUE

As Aristotle himself makes absolutely clear, such excellence can be understood in either of two senses. One is the kind of virtue or excellence that ordinary mortals can aspire to, which means, essentially, the virtues of conventional and unphilosophical people who are civilized rather than barbarous. What he is asking in that part of his discussion comes down to this: What is the standard that people of cultivated taste and refinement actually express in their feelings and actions? And his answer is that, with some qualifications and even with some exceptions, that standard is moderation. Clearly, that is not a very far-reaching ethical insight. One might even call Aristotle's reflections on the ordinary virtues banal, were it not for the thoroughness and subtlety of his analyses.

There is, however, *another* sense of virtue, alluded to by Aristotle as intellectual virtue. This turns out to be, exactly as we should expect, the perfection of individual excellence through the cultivation of reason. And it is, again, widely misunderstood by modern students of philosophy. Readers tend to think of the last book of Aristotle's *Ethics* as a kind of postscript or afterthought, as nothing more than superfluous and unessential praise for the philosopher's life. It is, on the contrary, the logical culmination and crown of his thought upon ethics.

Socrates had argued that human virtue is the fulfillment of one's function as a person. It would, indeed, be better to say that he took this for granted, for it is hardly a matter of argument in the Socratic dialogues. It is one of the few claims Socrates made that seems never to have been contested. To the Greeks it seemed obvious that the virtue of *anything* is the perfection of its function. And we think that way too. We suppose, as they did, that a good physician is one who performs well his function of healing, and a poor physician one who does it ineptly. When the Greeks thought of a bad physician, bad flute player, or bad anything, they did not mean, as moderns sometimes might, an *immoral* one, but an *incompetent* one. The goodness of such persons had little to do with their motives, but much to do with their abilities.

DUTY AND ASPIRATION

The concept of function was basic to the Greek way of thinking about philosophical ethics. But while we are perfectly familiar with that concept, we almost never apply it to ethics; and the reason is quite obvious. We think of ethics as having to do, not with a person's skills or abilities—or, in other words, with what he can *be*—but rather with his will or choices—or with what he can *do*. The Greeks thought of virtue as the perfection of a capacity, while we think of it as the possession of a benevolent will. Thus we would not—like the Greeks—think of a bumbling and incompetent physician who was doing his best, as a *bad* physician in any ethical sense but would apply that term instead to a physician, however skilled, who overcharged, or who refused to treat the poor, or who lied to his patients.

These are two very different ways of thinking of ethics. And when we apply our ethical point of view, which I have called the ethics of duty, based upon the idea of moral right and wrong, to the ethical writings of the Greeks that express an ethics of aspiration, then we not only distort the profound reflections of the ancients, but we also conceal from ourselves that very profundity.

Aristotle declares, in the opening book of his work, that it would be odd indeed to suppose that, while everything else has a proper function, a human being has none. Such a supposition seemed to him so glaringly false that it needed only to be stated for its absurdity to be apparent. The question, he supposed, was not whether a person has some unique and proper function but, rather, what that function is. And the answer to this seemed just as obvious to Aristotle as it had to Socrates: the perfection of the rational life. *That* is the key to Aristotle's reflections on ethics.

RATIONALITY AS THE SHARED ASPIRATION
OF THE ANCIENT MORALISTS

By now it should be clear that Aristotle was far from unique in praising the rational life. All the philosophical moralists of his culture did the same. The philosophies even of those who projected alternative ideals, like the Epicureans, cannot be properly understood except in terms of the seriousness with which they took this one. The Epicureans, for example, were seeking a rational life. They only denied that the cultivation of reason is itself the highest good, identifying this instead with pleasure. They asked what a wise and rational person would incorporate into his life in his quest for *eudaemonia*; and they answered that he would seek to increase for himself the only thing that is by nature good and to minimize the only natural evil, these being, respectively, pleasure and pain. The problem of the moralist was, they assumed, merely to discover the paths that lead to this goal. Never did the Epicureans discourse on the nature of moral right and wrong. They did not think in terms of that distinction. The nearest they came to this was to declare that, as a matter of experience, one could not live happily unless he also lived honorably and justly. But here, honor and justice are extolled merely as the means to happiness, and there is no hint that they are to be understood in any but a purely conventional sense. So here, as elsewhere among the ancient moralists, ethics is understood to rest not upon conscience or any kind of moral sense, and certainly not upon faith in a supreme lawmaker, but solely upon reason. The only basic issue between the ethical rationalists, such as Socrates and his great successors, and the more empirically-minded hedonists, was whether the rational life was itself the ideal to strive for, or whether it should be regarded as an instrument in the attainment of a good that could actually be felt, that is, pleasure.

Socrates' successors, starting from that same seemingly obvious foundation, concentrated almost exclusively on its ethical implications. The task of moral philosophy, they assumed, was to show that the perfection of reason, and its governance of conduct in both the individual and the state, was the only ultimate concern of the wise. Rationality is by nature a human being's unique and, hence, distinctive capacity. Its perfection is therefore our natural virtue or excellence. Conventional values, or the virtues and blessings that are the creations of culture, tended to be disregarded by most ancient moralists. The Cynics went farthest in this, going to great lengths to exhibit their contempt for all conventional virtue. The Stoic disdain for conventional goods was hardly less extreme. Even Plato was ready to jettison every conventional distinction of right and wrong that conflicted with his view of natural justice, conceived as the governance of the individual and of the *polis* by the rational element. Thus he did not hesitate to include women within the governing class, inasmuch as they possessed the same capacities for reason and the cultivation of philosophy as men, even though this was radically at odds with convention.

THE CONCEPT OF MORAL VIRTUE

Aristotle, in keeping with his philosophical tradition, makes clear his endorsement of the perfection of the rational life as a person's natural good, basing this on his presupposition concerning human uniqueness. But he does not pursue this idea forthwith, in total disregard of conventional ethics. Instead he puts it off for later consideration, meanwhile entering upon an analysis of the very conventional virtues that it was the practice of other moralists to scorn. He lumps these together as "moral virtue," that is, the ordinary excellences that are within reach of practical men of affairs who lack the inclination or incentive to pursue the ultimate virtue, aptly characterized by Aristotle as "intellectual."

And how does he resolve questions concerning conventional virtue? In much the same way that contemporary teachers of ethics do, by considering how persons of his own culture would react to them. Thus, in considering whether a given quality is a virtue, a vice, or neither, in effect he is simply asking how it would be regarded by the kind of person who is deemed virtuous in his own culture. This hardly differs from the common practice of contemporary academics of asking what "we would say" about some real or imagined situation. Thus, for example, a contemporary teacher of ethics is apt to pose the question of the degree of obligation one might have to return a borrowed book under various imagined conditions. Would one have an obligation to return it if one became ill; if one badly needed it and the owner had a duplicate copy; if returning it would somehow involve grave risks, and so on? And answers to such questions are found by considering what "we would say" about those imagined situations. Clearly, this is an appeal to the values that "we," people like ourselves, happen to hold. There is no thought of casting doubt upon those basic values themselves, nor is it at all clear what would count as confirming or disproving them. The fact that they are held, and held by all of "us," is considered sufficient for considering them to be real—which makes it worth noting again that the term "ethics," which is of Greek derivation, referred originally to nothing more pretentious than the habitual conduct of people "like us."

By such an approach, one can analyze conventional ethical concepts but nothing else. One can see the logical connections between such concepts, as they are conventionally employed. But one cannot show, nor even ask, whether such concepts have any validity apart from their general acceptance by persons who are deemed estimable by others of their own culture.

THE RELATIVE MEAN

The same holds for Aristotle's analyses of the conventional virtues and his discovery that "the relative mean" is exhibited in most of them—but significantly, not all of them. He was perfectly aware that he was, in those now famous sections of his book, dealing only with the conventional virtues of his culture. That is why he grouped them all together under the name "moral virtue," and carefully distinguished this from what was to come later, namely intellectual virtue, or what we can refer to, without any distortion at all, as natural virtue or even *real* virtue. We see, moreover, how very far Aristotle's conception of ethics was from the modern one when we note some of the qualities of character that he included among the virtues—a sense of humor, for example, a friendly disposition, a correct estimate of one's own worth, and so on. What, one is tempted to ask, has a sense of humor to do with *ethics*? Wit may be a charming and ingratiating characteristic, but one could hardly be morally blameworthy if he lacked it. Such responses would surely have bewildered Aristotle who might appropriately have asked what moral blameworthiness could possibly have to do with virtue or the lack of it.

PRIDE AS A VIRTUE

It may strike one as remarkable that Aristotle considers pride one of the moral virtues; but it is easy enough to see why. People are, of course, not born proud the way they are born male or female, nor do they become proud through the exercise of any natural capacity the way they become intelligent or physically strong. Furthermore, pride does not result from the cultivation of a single capacity but through the cultivation of many, some of which are natural and some not. For example, Aristotle thought that a proud person should be tall and possessed of a deep voice, even though neither is the product of training. On the other hand, the contempt that a proud person has for insignificant persons, the courage displayed in the face of danger, and the willingness to accept honors from worthy persons but not from inferior persons—these are all things that must be learned.

Again, pride is a mean between the extremes of humility and vanity, which clearly marks it as a conventional or "moral" virtue. For even though not all such virtues have the character of being a mean between two extremes—truth telling is one of the exceptions noted by Aristotle—all virtues that *do* exhibit this characteristic of moderation are conventional. There can be no such thing as excess with respect to any natural excellence, in the sense understood by the Greeks. If, for example, the perfection of a rational life is the natural excellence of a human being, as most ancient moralists believed, then it can make no sense to speak of excelling in this *by moderation*. A moderate degree of any natural virtue can be nothing but a fault, for here moderation can only mean mediocrity.

ARISTOTLE'S ETHICAL ELITISM

Aristotle's description of the proud man is so important that we should have it before us:

The proud man, since he deserves the grandest things, would be best. For the better man is always deserving of the grander, and the best of the grandest. It is therefore necessary that the truly proud man be good, and grandeur in each of the virtues would seem to belong to him. In no way would it be proper to the proud man to pump his arms when fleeing on foot, nor to do an injustice; for to what purpose would he do something disgraceful when there is nothing great in relation to him? . . . Pride, therefore, seems to be a certain comeliness, as it were, of the virtues. It makes them grander, and it cannot itself arise without them. It is because of this that it is difficult to be truly proud; for it is not possible without complete nobility and goodness. Now the proud man has very much to do with honor and dishonor. He will, on the one hand, be suitably pleased by the great honors bestowed by good men, on the grounds that they are only proper to him (or even less than proper, for there could not arise honor which is befitting complete virtue; yet he will accept it because they have nothing greater to offer him). But he will make light of all honor proffered for some small reason, and by any chance person, as being unbefitting. . . . Power and wealth are desirable for the honor they bring . . . and for him to whom even honor is trivial, so too are the other things. Whence proud men seem to be aloof. . . . And he is not apt to expose himself to trivial dangers . . . but rather for great causes only, and when he does so he gives no thought to his own life, believing that life at all costs is not worth having. He is the sort of man to confer benefits, but who feels shame when he himself is done a good turn; for the former is proper to one who excels, and the latter to a lesser man. When he is done a favor, he will repay it and more, for thus the original benefactor will be not only repaid, but himself be rendered favored and indebted. . . . And while a proud man needs nothing from others, or nearly nothing, he willingly renders service to others. And when he is with men of position and good fortune, he conducts himself with grandeur, but he is suitably moderate to those of mid-station. For to stand out from the former is a difficult and respected thing, but to outshine the latter is easy; and while a solemn bearing to the former is nothing ignoble, it becomes rather vulgar when displayed amongst the more humble—it is akin to bullying the weak. . . . It is necessary that he openly express his hatred or love, for to hide it is the mark of a timid man . . . and to speak and act openly, for he is outspoken because of his disregard for the opinion of others, and because of his truthfulness. . . . Neither is he prone to admiration; for nothing to him is great. . . . nor is he apt to malign others, not even his enemies, except for arrogance. . . . He is the sort to possess beautiful but profitless things rather than those which are fruitful and beneficial; for the former show self-reliance. And it would seem that an unhurried stride is proper to the proud man, along with a deep voice and a firm tone. . . . Such then, is the proud man . . . (1123^b–5^a).

This passage is usually regarded by contemporary readers as an aberration, or even a defacement, of Aristotle's otherwise clear and instructive moral insights. There is apt to be something of a wish that this great philosopher had not said these things. But something very characteristically Aristotelian would be missing from his book if this description were not there, namely the belief, which very few philosophers of antiquity questioned, that some people really are better than others and therefore count for more. Indeed this is inherent in the idea of aspiration itself, and no moral philosophy expresses an ethics of aspiration better than Aristotle's. If the purpose of moral philosophy is to delineate an ideal of human nature and to mark the path to its attainment, as the ancient moralists assumed, then we can hardly suppose that everyone, the wise and the foolish alike, attains it in equal measure. On the contrary, it is unlikely that any but a few ever achieve it at all, and these are literally *better* than the masses of persons who fall short. To try to understand the ancient classical moralists without presupposing this is like trying to understand the moral philosophy of Kant after expunging from it the idea of duty.

This elitism, the sharp and invidious distinction which Aristotle makes between people who are worthwhile and those who are not, is no incidental idiosyncrasy. It recurs in his somewhat labored treatment of the difficult question whether one can be a friend with a slave—someone he describes as nothing but a "living tool,"—as well as in his limitation of genuine friendship to those relatively few persons who are *good,* that is, who measure up to a refined standard of human excellence. And indeed, elitism is inherent in his whole conception of ethics. The most basic questions of ethics could not even arise for Aristotle if he were required to assume, in the face of all experience, that all persons are inherently or by nature *equal.* It was for him the very function of ethics to nourish and increase their inequality, to enable those who are naturally better to rise as far as possible above others with respect to individual worth. Indeed, if we had to suppose that all persons are by nature of equal worth, then what would be the point of talking about human goodness or virtue in the first place? Virtue is the perfection of function and if it is possessed merely by being a person—*any* person—then there is clearly nothing left to perfect.

Of course it is not difficult to see why the ancient and the modern views are so divergent here. We are the product of long religious and political traditions that were entirely unknown to Aristotle and his predecessors. Basic to that religious tradition is the doctrine of the inherent worth of each individual human being, expressed in the first book of the Bible in terms of the metaphor of God's image. It culminates, in the New Testament, in the claim that it is the meek and the humble who are blessed, who are the very salt of the earth—claims that would have seemed to Aristotle, and to every other philosophical moralist of antiquity, not only laughably absurd but a dangerous inversion of values. Our political tradition, which cannot be considered independent of the religious one, also rests upon the presupposition that all persons are by nature of equal worth. But if the presuppositions of these traditions are correct—if the least among us is as good as the best, and if such equality is natural instead of conventional—then almost the whole of ancient moral philosophy is reduced to nonsense. And Aristotle's ethics, to say the least, is rendered as dull and pointless as it is apt to seem to readers upon their initiation to it, readers who are not automatically charmed by the kind of pedestrian philosophical analysis at which Aristotle excelled.

INTELLECTUAL VIRTUE AS AN ASPIRATION

Once the modern reader penetrates the veil of prejudice that our cultural traditions have created and sees that Aristotle really does mean what he says about pride and the natural superiority of some few over the many, then he is able to see the philosopher's description of intellectual virtue in its true light. This occurs in Book VI and again at the end of the work, in Book X. Readers are apt to treat Aristotle's praise of the rational and contemplative life as a kind of afterthought or postscript, something superfluously added and not essential to the main themes of the book. It is, however, the culmination of the work and, probably, as philosophically important and serious as any of the themes Aristotle develops.

What Aristotle is saying is essentially this: There are many rules, customs, virtues, values, and norms essential to civilized life. They are of human origin—Aristotle seems never to have doubted this—but nevertheless of interest to philosophy. They include the customary human virtues, which Aristotle analyzes with such care, as well as the traditional notions of justice, friendship, and so on. A proper understanding of all these things is necessary for a good life. No one can hope for a good life if he has no proper understanding of honor, for example, or of justice, for he will then resemble an animal or a barbarian more than a civilized person.

But the understanding of all these things, while it is necessary to a good life, will not bless one with the highest life. For this, one must go beyond conventional values and seek what is the natural human good. And how does one do that? Not by analyzing common ethical ideas, but by perfecting the natural function of a human being. This is, of course, assumed to be the exercise of the rational faculty.

This illation was the foundation of Socratic ethics and, as we have seen, of the moral philosophies that derived their inspiration from Socrates—which means, virtually all the moral philosophy of antiquity, especially Plato's. No one, however, expressed it more clearly than Aristotle, in these straightforward passages:

> Just as for a flute player, or sculptor, or any artist (and generally for anything which has some function or activity) the *good* or the *excellent* seems to reside in that function, so too it would seem to be for *man*, if indeed he has some function. Now, would a carpenter and a shoemaker have their functions and activities, and yet *man* have none? Does he have no natural work? Or rather, just as the eye, and the hand, and the foot, and in general each of his parts evidently has its function, must we not posit a function for *man* over and above all of these? What then would this be? It seems that he shares the act of living

even with plants, whereas the object of our search is that which is peculiar to *man*; we must therefore reject a life of simple nutrition and growth. Next would be the perceptual life, but this is shared with horses, oxen, and indeed every animal. What remains, then, is a life characterized by the activity of that which has reason . . . (1097^{b}–8^{a}).

These lines appear at the beginning of his work, and the final book, devoted to the contemplative life, is simply Aristotle's inference from them, following the lengthy detour into "moral" virtue and the various concepts of conventional values. Aristotle could have, following the pattern of the Cynics and Stoics, gone from his opening reflections upon the natural function of a person straight to the description of "intellectual" virtue and the contemplative life, dismissing everything in between as merely conventional and therefore of little philosophical interest. This would have been an immense omission, and much of value would have been lost, but his work would nevertheless have retained a unity and completeness. If, on the other hand, the description of intellectual virtue had been omitted, then the work would have been essentially incomplete, like a syllogism that lacks a conclusion.

The description of the contemplative life is the description of a life that is ideal by nature. It is the ultimate good. Its goodness is not the result of anything conferred by people. It is not a life of honor, wealth, glory, or power. All these are good, but they are good only by human standards. They are conventionally good. A life devoted to reason, that is, to the increase of knowledge and the exercise of one's natural function, is good by nature.

Thus Aristotle is not, as one is tempted to suppose, merely praising the kind of life he himself happened to enjoy. When he says that the life of philosophy is the life most closely akin to that of the gods, he is not merely indulging in hyperbole. He is drawing the logical conclusion from his analysis of a human being's unique function and natural excellence. It is necessary to remember, however, that for Aristotle, the pursuit of philosophy was one and the same as the general pursuit of knowledge and wisdom.

ARISTOTLE'S INCOMPARABLE GREATNESS

The *Nicomachean Ethics* represents Aristotle's attempt to divide the entire subject of ethics into the two great categories that were generally taken for granted by ancient moralists, namely into those things that are true by convention, sometimes aptly called "vulgar" virtue, and those that are true by nature and that constitute true virtue, and then to analyze them all. It was an attempt that was immensely successful. Unlike many of his predecessors, he did not place nature and convention in opposition to each other. He simply treated them as different.

Modern readers of his incomparable work tend to take most seriously the analyses of conventional concepts, especially the description of the virtues. When one thinks of Aristotelian ethics, one is likely to think first of the idea of moderation, as if this more or less expresses the basic idea of the book. In fact, however, its essential idea is *im*moderation, that is, a kind of perfection of the intellectual aspect of human nature of which few persons are capable. The idea of moderation is suitable enough for the ordinary virtues, but it is no ordinary virtue that Aristotle ultimately praises.

That intellectual excellence is a natural virtue and not a mere conventional one follows from the fact that it derives from the natural function of a person. Human beings are not rational simply because they deem themselves to be so, in the way that they are "equal" in modern democracies just because they declare themselves such. Human beings are by nature rational, that is, possessed of the capacities for an intellectual life. No other creature is. Nor, of course, are all persons possessed of this capacity in equal degree. It is nevertheless, to whatever degree possessed, a gift of nature, not of acculturation.

This idea of natural function is almost never found in the writings of modern moralists. For them, it is almost as if this great tradition, the flowering of moral philosophy, had never existed. Human beings are, of course, almost invariably assumed by modern writers to be rational; but the Aristotelian inference that some persons can therefore become naturally better than others, and that genuine virtue consists of doing just that, is never drawn. Instead, following Kant and virtually every other modern moralist, it is supposed that by this rationality we can, all of us including the most ignorant and stupid, draw some presumed distinction between moral right and wrong! Kant even supposed that his great "categorical imperative" was within the ken of any untutored peasant! No ancient moralist, especially Aristotle, could have taken such a suggestion seriously nor even really have understood it. It should, however, be noted that the basic claim of modern writers such as Kant has to do with *moral* right and wrong, not just customary right and wrong. The latter is, of course, within the ken of any person capable of absorbing the mores of his culture, as no ancient moralist doubted.

This reorientation of moral philosophy, away from the ideal of personal excellence and in favor of the concept of duty, has been so thoroughgoing that it has become difficult for contemporary thinkers even to understand the idea of human goodness in the way the ancients understood it. We think of virtue as mere integrity, as simple adherence to moral principle, often as consisting of nothing more than blamelessness. The tribute to some person, that he leads a blameless life, is considered to be about the same as a tribute to his virtue. Hence Aristotle's frequent references to a "good man," as in the description of pride quoted earlier, is almost always completely misunderstood. There, for example, he says at the outset that "the truly proud man must be good." We imagine that he is alluding to someone who is fair, decent and honest—"good," in the moral sense that we attach to the word. He is saying, rather, that a proud man must be something extraordinary, far above the ordinary run who manage to be no more than fair, decent, and honest. Similarly, he declares that genuine friendship, of the highest kind, can exist only between persons who are "good" or "virtuous." We imagine that he means persons who are, in *our* sense of the term, virtuous, and we have no difficulty imagining that this kind of friendship might exist between the perfectly ordinary people we encounter every day—between day laborers, or businessmen, or members of a garden club. We imagine, in other words, that Aristotle is referring to people who *act* in certain approved ways in their dealings with others, and we have no difficulty whatsoever in imagining that such goodness might be possessed by the meek, the humble, and even the ignorant, a supposition that to Aristotle would have been self-contradictory. Indeed, we do not find it difficult to suppose that a slave could be a "good man," which would surely have been incomprehensible to Aristotle. When Aristotle described a person as *good,* he meant, *good as a person,* that is, singular or outstanding with respect to the uniquely human capacity for intellectual excellence. Such goodness is reserved for the few. Aristotle's graphic and lengthy description of the exemplar of virtue, the proud man, says virtually nothing about what that good man *does.* Instead, it describes what he *is.*

Aristotle's ethics, with its emphasis upon aspiration to an ideal of human nature, is thus paradigmatic of the moral philosophies of the ancients. All portrayed an ideal for individual attainment and, in virtually all of them, that ideal was represented as a rational life. The ancients were, to be sure, concerned with how people ought to treat each other, but questions of that kind were not thought by them, as they are by us, to be central to ethics. The central question was always: What shall I strive to become in order to achieve the kind of existence that I am meant to have as a person? And the answer was, usually, a rational being. Happiness was almost invariably assumed to be, not some kind of *reward* for that achievement, as though the achievement were itself something onerous and therefore deserving of compensation. Rather, it was thought to *consist* of being that kind of person.

It is a very ancient ideal, and was carried into the Roman world by the Stoics. The writings of the Stoics emphasize the idea of duty, to be sure, but this is represented as being primarily duty to oneself. It is in fact simply the duty to be rational. And of course the ideal of rationality, or at least the cultivation of intellectual pursuit, still persists. What has changed is that this is no longer considered to have much to do with ethics. Modern philosophical moralists praise rationality, to be sure, but few would declare that persons who do not make the cultivation of reason central to their lives are thereby lacking in moral goodness. Instead, they suppose that reason will serve as a guide to a different end altogether, namely the discernment of the distinction between moral right and wrong. This represents a complete reorientation of philosophical ethics. What produced it, as we shall see, was the rise of the Christian church with its emphasis not on reason but on faith, and its claim that no person can stand higher than any other in terms of any inherent worth, the very least of persons being every bit as "good" as the best.

chapter 11

The Foundation
of the Ethics of Duty

The result, for ethics, of the rise and spread of Christianity was not merely the replacement of pagan ideals by others. It was much more far-reaching. It was in fact an entirely new way of looking at ethics, and one that still constitutes the framework of both popular and philosophical ethics even for those who imagine that their thinking is in no way conditioned by religion.

What happened, in a word, is that the idea of moral right and wrong replaced that of personal excellence. This idea of right and wrong is still so central to ethics that most philosophers never doubt its relevance to that subject, however skeptical some of them may be concerning its applicability. The old idea of virtue, or personal excellence, has in the meantime almost vanished as a concept of philosophical ethics. Indeed, as we have noted, it is no longer even understood. Philosophers themselves assume that virtue must be something intimately connected with morally right conduct. Here, the effect of religion has been so overwhelming as to permanently condition the thinking even of philosophers who rest their opinions on reason, and who are the traditional foes of believers who rest theirs upon faith.

Of course no one would suggest that the ideas of right and wrong were unfamiliar to the ancients, prior to the rise of Christianity. Among the Greeks, as we have seen, it was a distinction that was taken for granted. The contribution of the Christian religion was to lift the distinction between right and wrong, which was originally a man-made one reflecting purely human needs, to the level of *moral* right and wrong. This was considered to be a real distinction, higher than anything that is purely human and hence conventional. Distinctions of moral right and wrong came to be regarded originally as expressing the will of God, not human will and purpose.

THE PRACTICAL BASIS OF THE ETHICS OF CUSTOM

The basic ideas of right and wrong are of course familiar to every culture for they are absolutely essential to any kind of social life. The original idea of *wrong* is that of something forbidden, while *right* is something permitted. And that which is *obligatory* is required. Every society must distinguish between those things that are and are not permitted, as a condition of its very existence. People cannot live together in peace and security if there are no prohibitions of actions that threaten life, peace, and security. Thus arise all the basic prohibitions, essentially the same in every society, of behavior that threatens the elementary requirements of social life. Indeed, the connection between the fundamental prohibitions that all societies respect and teach or, in other words, what are everywhere considered "wrongs," and the practical social needs that these prohibitions tend to protect, is almost too obvious to belabor.

Closely connected with the idea of what is forbidden is that of what is required or, in ethical terms, "obligatory." The idea of a prohibition is of course negative, and it is no accident that most codes of morality have the same character, expressed as "thou shalt *not*." Social life first of all requires that people exercise *restraint*. They must *abstain* from certain actions that would threaten the social structure. But positively, there are also some things that ought to be done, so that people may not only live in peace, but that they may flourish and prosper. And this requires that they not simply abstain from what is hurtful, but that they positively do what is beneficial—for example, that they defend the group against its enemies, hold some sort of allegiance to that group and its ruling persons, pay taxes to them, and so on.

That is obviously where all right and wrong begin, in the protection and fostering of those human needs that are seen to be essential to the social life that human beings can hardly live without. Some things have to be forbidden, others required; the rest are merely permitted. The first class of things is then referred to as wrong, the second as obligatory, and the rest as right, in the minimal sense of acceptable.

From these elementary reflections two things at once become apparent. The first is that the original distinctions of right, wrong, and obligatory are of human origin. No gods are needed, and certainly no philosophers, in order for people to see what kinds of actions must be forbidden and what kinds required if they are to live together and flourish. And the second idea, even more obvious than the first, is that these distinctions are overwhelmingly important and are made no less so by their human origin. That a given people should be able to live together in safety from each other is as important to them as anything could be. It is important to life itself, since life depends on it. Having thus secured minimal safety by banning hurtful actions as wrong, it is then important to them, not merely to live, but to thrive. And for this, certain classes of actions, less numerous than those that are prohibited, come to be required, or obligatory.

Here we have the rudiments of ethics, or of those patterns of conduct that are mutually expected within a given group, that is, by "people like us," which is the original root meaning of *ethnos*. Distinctions of conduct are made, but they are not absolute; and they are related to human aims and purposes. Indeed, they are entirely derivative from those aims and purposes. The distinctions are "taught," in the sense of being imparted, this being the major element in the acculturation of anyone belonging to that particular group. And while the ethical distinctions thus arising are not absolute, there is nevertheless a basic resemblance from one culture to another, explained by the fact that the needs and goals of people are similar everywhere, especially the need for safety of life and limb. The conditions of life differ from one place to another giving rise to differences, and differences of emphasis, with respect to what is forbidden and what required; but the ethical distinctions themselves, and the moral codes that embody them, everywhere arise from an identical source, which is human needs and purposes.

THE RELATIONAL CHARACTER OF ETHICAL TERMS

We must next note that the ideas of prohibiting, permitting, and requiring are ideas expressing certain relationships of a person or persons to others. Nothing, for example, is simply "permitted," "forbidden," or "required." These are expressions of relationship, just as obviously as such expressions as "to the left of" and "larger." A given action is permitted, forbidden, or required *of* certain persons *by* other persons. Those other persons can, of course, be the other members of a given group—a family, tribe, *polis*, nation, or some person or group within that larger group, a king, or a priesthood, or whoever is thought of as having ruling authority. Typically, the ideas of ethical right and wrong, that is, of permission and prohibition, express the dominant relationship of an entire people or culture over its individual members. Thus, a given "ethnos," or more or less culturally homogeneous group, forbids some things, permits others, and requires still others, and these expectations are instilled in the individual members. The patterns of behavior thus expected are then seen as the "ethics" of that culture.

Similar observations can be made concerning the ideas of *duty* and *obligation.* A duty is something that is owed, something *due,* and to be obligated is, literally, to be *bound.* But something can be owed only *to* some person or persons. There can be no such thing as a duty in isolation, that is, something that is owed but owed to no person or persons. Similarly, one can have no obligation just as such; it must, again, be an obligation to some person or persons, for the idea of being bound or tied, yet bound to no one or no thing, is without meaning. Duties and obligations always arise from relationships between persons. Typically, for example, a servant has certain duties to a master, an employee to an employer, a citizen to a country, a soldier to a commander, and so on. Typically, again, such relationships are mutual, though what is thus owed by each to the other is usually different. Thus, an employee owes or is obligated to render to an employer certain labor; and the employer has a similar duty to render payment. Parents are obligated to their children and children to their parents, but again in different ways, the first owing protection and the other obedience, and so on.

Such relationships arise in all sorts of contexts, but the thing to bear in mind is that they are always relationships. No one can have a duty that is not a duty *to* anyone; and the same is true of obligation. In its original ethical sense, duty was characteristically thought of as duty to one's own people, that is, to people like oneself or of the same culture. As people have become closer and their cultures have tended to merge, the idea has developed that each of us has certain obligations to any and all persons, that is, not just to group, or nation, or persons narrowly "like ourselves" but to the whole of humankind. But the thing to bear in mind is that obligation is still thought of, even in this expanded ethical sense, as owed *to* some person or persons—even if that should happen to include all persons, born and unborn.

ARE ETHICAL CONCEPTS ALL "RELATIVE"?

If the ideas of permission, prohibition, requirement, owing, and being bound, together with the ethical concepts that arise from them—namely, those of right, wrong, obligatory, and so on—are all relational, expressing certain relationships between persons and groups, shall we then conclude that all ethics is relative? In a sense, yes, but only in a very restricted sense. Ethical distinctions arise entirely from human needs and purposes, and are in that sense relative to these, but they are not relative in any other sense. They are not, for example, arbitrary, nor unimportant, which is usually what is implied in calling them "relative"; nor are they to be heeded or disregarded as one pleases. They are absolutely necessary for social life, and for people who live in societies as virtually all people do, some are necessary even for life itself. To say, then, that distinctions of right and wrong are all "just relative," in the sense of being unimportant and to be disregarded as one pleases, would amount to saying that life is unimportant and to be treated casually. No one believes that, at least so far as his own life is concerned. At the same time, one can hardly fail to see the importance of certain prohibitions in protecting life, so in that sense, the relative character of ethics should be obvious to everyone. Moral laws were not inscribed by God in the skies, nor on stone tablets. Their source is far more obvious. They were fashioned over the generations by human beings living in societies and quite naturally concerned for their personal safety and well-being.

This was taken for granted by the Greeks prior to the rise of Christianity. Even Socrates, who sometimes spoke as if the concepts of ethics and justice stood by themselves, fixed in their meanings and unconnected with human needs, nevertheless still thought of obligation as essentially political. The Socratic dialogue that best exhibits his conception of duty is probably the *Crito.* And what needs to be noticed about that dialogue is that Socrates describes his ultimate obligation, the highest obligation he could think of, not as a duty to the gods or to any abstract principle, but as a duty to *the laws.* He does, to be sure, dramatically personify those laws, describing how they have nourished and taught him, almost as if they were gods or parents, but this is essentially rhetorical and dramatic. Socrates could hardly have doubted that the laws of the Athenians, to which he alludes and to which he bows, were the creations of the Athenians. And he simply took for granted in that dialogue that duty is necessarily duty *to* some person or persons—in this case, to the *polis,* which had expressed its requirements and its prohibitions in its laws. He does not suggest that, the laws having condemned him to death, he has a simple and abstract duty to remain and accept that punishment. He represents it as a bargain he has struck and must now abide by, even when the agreement he has made goes against him. But bargains and agreements are made between persons, and duties that arise under them are duties to persons, not just duties as such. Socrates personifies the laws as if they were persons and speaks as though his duty were to those laws, which is a nice and philosophical way of expressing the concept of duty in this context. Still, it is represented as duty *to* persons or, in this case, to things personified. It is, in other words, still relational and essentially political. It is not represented by Socrates as a religious duty, obviously, nor as an abstract one (as if duty could be something other than a relationship).

chapter 12

Religion and the Concept of Moral Obligation

The rise and spread of Christianity had immense and far-reaching effects upon the ethical thought of our culture. It was not just popular ethics nor the thinking of the adherents of this religion that were affected, nor was it just that new ethical ideals arose. This religion also altered forever the direction of philosophical ethics in ways not always apparent to philosophers. Thus, when one considers, for example, the ethical writings of J. S. Mill or Immanuel Kant, the influence of religion may not be immediately apparent. That is because, while the answers are not drawn from religion, the basic questions still are. Philosophy has, in other words, retained the basic conception of ethics inherited from religion, while abandoning the presuppositions that made it meaningful.

Two ways in which this happened stand out. The first is the replacement of the traditional idea of obligation with a new one, henceforth to be thought of as *moral* obligation. The second is the virtual obliteration of the traditional ideal of virtue, conceived as personal excellence, upon which most moral philosophy had hitherto rested.

These effects were long-lasting, and even now condition virtually all of philosophical ethics. It is, for example, almost impossible to find any serious philosophical treatment of this subject which does not simply *presuppose* the legitimacy of speaking of moral obligations. And it is almost as rare to find any serious discussion of ethics in which the idea of virtue has not been entirely divested of the meaning it had for the philosophers before the rise of Christianity.

THE IDEA OF MORAL OBLIGATION

Religion, and more specifically the Christian religion, nourished the idea that there is a kind of obligation higher, more authoritative, and more demanding than the obligations that arise among persons, higher even than one's obligation to the state, or to humanity itself—namely, obligation or duty to God. Thus arose the idea of a unique kind of obligation, which eventually came to be called *moral* obligation, hitherto quite unknown to philosophy. What is demanded of us by God, it came to be believed, takes precedence over anything demanded of one person by another, even if the latter is a king or a Caesar. And philosophers, even though they no longer think of ethics in religious terms still, to this day, consider it meaningful to speak of a kind of moral obligation that is supposed to take precedence over every other. It is no longer thought of as an obligation to God, to be sure; indeed, it is no longer thought of as an obligation *to* any person or persons, divine or other. It is simply thought of as a unique obligation that each of us has, standing by itself. Whether this idea of moral obligation has any meaning, independent of the concept of God from which it was originally inseparable, can be doubted, but we leave consideration of that point for later discussion.

THE ECLIPSE OF THE CONCEPT OF VIRTUE

The second effect of the rise and spread of Christianity was the almost total destruction of the Greek ideal of personal excellence, considered as an ethical ideal. For it was not, as we have seen, merely that the Greeks prized individual excellence. It was the very foundation of their moral philosophy. It was the original meaning of virtue. The replacement of pagan ethics by Christian ethics was therefore not just the substitution of one ideal for another, nor the substitution of one concept of duty for another. It was the destruction of a whole approach to and framework of philosophical ethics. *It was the replacement of the ethics of aspiration with the ethics of duty.*

This second effect of religion, this complete reorientation of moral philosophy, was in turn the product of two things that lay at the foundation of the new religious influence: the idea of human worth and the replacement of reason by faith.

HUMAN WORTH

The new religion introduced to the Greek and Roman world the idea, as old as the Judeo-Christian tradition itself, that every person is of great and immeasurable worth, a veritable image of God, and that accordingly, *all* persons are of the same worth in the eyes of God. These claims are still, of course, warmly endorsed, even by persons having no belief in God, and we have become so accustomed to hearing them that they are no longer even thought of as having a religious origin. Any philosopher, as well as any clergyman or politician can proclaim the unique worth of every human being, and the resulting equality of all, and these grandiose claims, which would have seemed laughable to the Greeks, are apt to be received as surely true. Sometimes this alleged equality of all persons is even seriously proposed as self-evident, although the slightest reflection suggests that it is obviously not true if literally construed.

FAITH

The second fundamental claim of religion, and one that went to the very heart of Greek moral philosophy, was its assertion of the supremacy of faith *as a virtue*. The pagan moralists, however great may have been the differences among them, were almost unanimous in extolling the rational life as the ultimate virtue. Not only did they rest ethics upon the idea of aspiration rather than duty, what they held out as the object of that aspiration was the very thing that would come to stand diametrically opposed to the ideal of faith, namely reason.

This influence of religion upon western philosophy, which is seldom sufficiently appreciated, needs now to be looked at more closely.

THE CONCEPT OF MORAL OBLIGATION

People seem to have little difficulty thinking of a kind of obligation or duty that goes beyond any of the obligations that are created and dissolved by people, including those that are most time-honored and widely recognized. Thus, few persons would find any difficulty in supposing that honoring a trust, for example, or keeping a promise secretly made to someone now dead, might be morally obligatory, even though not legally so. Here the supposition is that we all have certain duties or obligations that no one has imposed upon us, that we have not voluntarily taken upon ourselves, and that are accordingly not obligations *to* anyone. Indeed, many would deem this self-evident in the case of some supposed obligations such as the general obligation each of us has to be truthful. These, it is supposed, are not obligations that can be created and abolished at will or even by mutual consent. They are binding *upon* us, yet they bind us *to* no persons; for that reason, it is supposed, we cannot be released from them. They are simply obligations to do what is "right."

This kind of higher obligation was once thought of as a duty to one's people, culture, or simply to one's *polis*. One had, it was thought, an ultimate obligation to obey *the laws,* these encompassing all the rules and customs, written or unwritten, governing conduct in a given culture. If someone were to enter into agreement with someone else to do something contrary to the laws—for instance, to evade a punishment lawfully imposed—then, it was supposed, such agreement would be deemed conspiratorial and wrong. That was precisely Socrates' reason for refusing to enter into Crito's scheme to effect his escape, even though he knew that his judges would have welcomed this alternative to putting him to death. It was thought that duty and obligation were defined by the laws and could not be abrogated, even by the voluntary and mutual consent of the parties affected by them.

But of course we must again remind ourselves that the laws, as thus conceived—that is, the rules governing the behavior of a given culture or political entity, whether written or unwritten—are conventional. They are the creations of the culture or, sometimes, of certain great leaders and lawmakers within that culture. Duty and obligation are likewise, under this conception, conventional concepts. One's ultimate duty is *to* certain persons, perhaps even to all persons. It is not a duty to any god or gods. The gods were not usually thought of as the authors of the laws, and the violation of law was not normally thought of as rebelling against the will of any god. The king might order something, and this order might have the force of law; but if his subjects refuse to obey, they are, in violating the law, defying only *him* and the laws and traditions under which he rules. They are not defying the gods. And similarly, established custom, perhaps as old as the culture that embodies it, might require certain actions such as defense of the state against its enemies. This, then, will be looked upon as a duty—in this case, a duty to the state. So if anyone refuses to perform that duty, he violates no *divine* command but only a law or custom of his state, however venerable that custom may be.

Christianity, however, emphasized the idea of an obligation that is higher than any that the ancient philosophical moralists had ever seriously entertained, and one that is *not* merely conventional. It introduced to them the idea of a duty to God which might be in conflict with their duty even to the state or to their culture. The idea of having obligations to the gods was not, of course, entirely new, but it had rarely been seriously thought that such a duty could be higher than duty to the state, or that divine commands might be in conflict with what everyone assumed to be his political obligations.

RELIGION AND NATURAL LAW

It is in this way that religion, somewhat paradoxically, gave a clearer meaning to the Socratic conception of a natural justice. It is paradoxical because the Greek idea of *nature* came to be assimilated into the idea of the *supernatural* fostered by religion.

Here, in very broad outline, is how that happened. Philosophers at about the time of Socrates, as we have seen, drew the distinction between that which is true merely by convention—that is, which is made true by the actions, pronouncements, and declarations of people—and that which is true independently of people. This latter they called nature. That which is true by nature they considered unalterably true. It is what we must bow to and accept but can never hope to change.

They then raised the question whether ethical distinctions, or what we would call the rules of morality, are merely conventional or natural. If all laws and customs are the inventions of human beings, then, no matter how valuable or even indispensable they may be, they are nevertheless conventional, raising the skeptical question whether we have any real obligation to heed them. But if, on the other hand, some of them are natural, then the obligations they impose are not just obligations imposed on human beings. They are absolute obligations and binding upon us, even when what they require is in violation of the oldest and most venerable laws and customs.

The ancient moralists—epitomized, for example, in the Stoics—thought more in terms of natural virtue rather than natural duty, as we have seen. They recognized but one supreme law and that was simply the command to live according to nature. With the spread of Christianity, however, and with it the idea of a god who is a supreme lawmaker, the idea was planted in Greek and Roman culture of a duty to that god which takes precedence over every duty to any person or persons. The laws of that god thus came to be thought of as the requirements of nature, in the *original* sense of the term; that is, they are binding obligations which have their source in no human will, and can, therefore, not be set aside by any human action. Natural justice was always thought of, by those philosophers who had a clear idea of it, as a kind of justice that is higher than human, and unalterable. The Commandments of God, as represented by the Christian church, fit exactly the same description. And thus was the Greek concept of nature carried over into the ethical framework introduced by religion, and paradoxically, identified with the laws and commandments of God, conceived as the creator of nature itself.

The process of assimilation seems somewhat confusing now, but it need not if we keep two things clearly before us. The first is that nature was not thought of by the Greeks as something opposed to the divine or supernatural but, rather, as something opposed to the merely human. And the second is that the central idea of moral philosophy, for the Greeks, was not moral obligation or duty, but virtue. If, accordingly, the Greek conception of obligation, which was invariably thought of as conventional—that is, as obligation to persons and created by persons—comes to be assimilated to the conception of obligation to God, that is, to a supreme lawgiver; and if then the concept of duty replaces the concept of virtue as the central one in ethics, the inevitable result is going to be the emergence of the idea of natural *law,* to replace that of natural virtue, and then the identification of this law with the laws of God.

It is for these reasons that classical writers in English jurisprudence, such as Austin and Blackstone, automatically equated natural law with the commands of God, and it is significant that they did not call it supernatural law. There must, they thought, be certain and fixed and eternal principles of law that are binding on all persons everywhere and that are, accordingly, higher or more authoritative than any human laws. And this, of course, very much expresses the basic idea of nature, as conceived by the pagan philosophers. But it also fits exactly the idea of divine laws as conceived in Christian theology.

Thus, in 1832, John Austin, the paradigm of legal positivists, wrote that "the whole or a portion of the laws set by God to men is frequently styled the law of nature, or natural law: being, in truth, the only natural law of which it is possible to speak without a metaphor." (*Province of Jurisprudence Determined,* Lecture I, 1832.) Sir William Blackstone, similarly, without even deeming it necessary to defend the claim, wrote that "this law of nature, being coeval with mankind, and dictated by God himself, is of course superior in obligation to any other;" to which he added that "it is binding over all the globe in all countries, and at all times," and that "no human laws are of any validity, if contrary to this; and such of them as are valid derive all their force and all their authority, mediately or immediately, from this original." (*Commentaries on the Laws of England,* Book I, 1860.) The fact that natural law was first thought of, in antiquity, as discoverable by reason rather than by faith was dealt with by Austin by attributing the gift of reason itself to God, thus making it possible to say that this law comes from both God *and* reason. Other moralists, such as Paley, came to refer to reason as "the light of nature," uniting two ideas into a single metaphor.

MORAL OBLIGATION AS AN EMPTY IDEA

It is thus from the amalgamation of ancient philosophical and religious ideas that the concept of moral obligation originated. Philosophers today do not, with rare exceptions, take very seriously the idea that morality must ultimately be identified with the requirements laid upon us by God, and they have, again with rare exceptions, all but forgotten the ancient distinction between natural and conventional justice. But they do take very seriously indeed the idea that is the offspring of these ancient conceptions, namely the idea of moral obligation and the distinction between moral right and wrong that it gives rise to. Indeed, it is everywhere assumed that the concept of moral obligation, and the correlative concepts of moral right and wrong, constitute the very subject matter of philosophical ethics. Philosophy has opened its door to this ill-conceived and misbegotten offspring of ancient philosophy and religion without a moment's inquiry into parentage; and it has made such a comfortable home for it now that philosophical ethics, grown old and tired, seems unable to take a single step without leaning on this adored child for support.

For what is the idea of moral obligation in modern philosophical thinking? It is the idea of an obligation that every responsible person is supposed to have, and yet it is an obligation to no person or persons. It is not an obligation to the state, nor to society in general, nor to the whole of humanity, nor even to God. It is just an obligation, standing all by itself, binding on all persons but not binding them *to* anything that exists. It is a presumed obligation to do what is "right", and by the same token to avoid what is "wrong." And these two terms, in turn, are either not defined at all or defined differently by different philosophers according to their own idiosyncrasies and predilections. Originally, however, *right* meant permitted by this or that person or group (by the state, for example); *wrong* meant forbidden; and *obligatory* meant required. Later, with the spread of Christianity into the world where rational philosophy had flourished, these terms came to mean permitted, forbidden, and required by God. But then, as belief in God faded, at least among philosophers, the *terms* right and wrong and obligatory were kept, though now divorced from any connection with any lawgiver, such as the state or God, which had given them their original meaning. And now, divested of their original relationship to any lawgiver, these words are simply prefixed by the word *moral,* similarly left undefined; as if merely adding one undefined philosophical term to another will produce meaning.

The idea of political or legal obligation is clear enough, for it is defined by the laws, and the laws in turn originate with identifiable human lawmakers. Similarly, the idea of an obligation higher than this, and referred to as *moral* obligation, is clear enough, provided reference to some lawmaker higher or more authoritative than those of the state is understood. In other words, our moral obligations can, in this manner, be understood as those that are imposed by God. This does give a clear sense to the claim that our moral obligations are more binding upon us than our political obligations, so that in case of conflict between the two, it is the latter that must yield. But what if this higher-than-human lawgiver is no longer taken into account? Does the concept of a moral obligation, more binding than any political, or otherwise humanly-imposed obligation, still make any sense? Do we, in fact, still mean anything at all in calling certain obligations *moral,* to distinguish them from lesser kinds? The fact that we *talk* that way, together with the fact that the most sophisticated philosophers can discourse at length with each other, using this pair of terms along with the correlative terms *morally right* and *morally wrong,* does not by itself indicate that they are speaking with any meaning at all. Sometimes terms, once meaningful, cease to be so, by being divested of the very conditions that gave them meaning; but they are still kept, along with many of the associations they once had. And these terms, everywhere considered to be so basic to philosophical as well as to popular ethics, appear to be perfect examples of this.

It is worth reminding ourselves again that the great classical moralists of antiquity whose thinking on matters of ethics has probably never been excelled or even equaled had no need for the concepts of moral right and wrong, or moral obligation, as they figure in modern philosophy. The ancients knew what they meant by justice, and by right and wrong as defined in terms of that concept. And the Romans who came under the influence of Christianity had a clear idea of a kind of obligation that was higher than any imposed even by the state. The mingling of these two influences has produced the idea of moral obligation, and the correlative ideas of moral right and wrong. But just as the ancient concept of virtue is unintelligible apart from the idea of function, so is the concept of moral obligation unintelligible apart from the idea of God. The words remain, but their meaning is gone.

chapter 13

The Destruction
of the Ideal of Virtue

The absorption of Christianity into western culture not only altered the traditional ideas of obligation, it utterly destroyed the pagan ideal of virtue, conceived as personal excellence. The destruction was so complete that the idea finds no place in modern philosophical ethics except in debased forms. The gulf that separates us from the pure and rational wisdom of the ancient philosophical moralists is not just one of time. It is an intellectual gulf, a corruption of basic ideas that distorts that ancient wisdom to the point that it is now hardly even understood. How else could a modern reader study Aristotle's ethical philosophy without realizing that it is fundamentally antithetical to some of the very foundations of contemporary ethical thought? And how else could anyone find in Socratic and Platonic philosophy an adumbration of democratic ideals?

PRIDE VERSUS HUMILITY

Aristotle upheld pride as perhaps the noblest of the moral virtues, a pride that is as rare as the personal excellence it rests upon. The new religion proclaimed the very opposite, that it is the meek and the humble who are blessed. To capture the contrast in a graphic image, we can say that the ignorant and uncouth, whom the proud Greeks would have dismissed as the scum of the earth, were suddenly proclaimed to be the salt of the earth. Those conditions of humanity that the ancient moralists had, with one voice, dismissed as unworthy of consideration—namely, humility, meekness, and ignorance—were all of a sudden declared to be virtues. Even the Cynics' scorn for worldly things was never a courting of humility, for their pride showed through the very rags that were their uniform. When Diogenes bade Alexander, the great king, to get out of his sunlight, it was not because he believed he had found favor in the eyes of any gods but simply because he deemed himself wiser and hence better than kings. He needed no gods to give him worth and no rules to give him virtue. Socrates had deemed it obvious that a person can have no more serious vocation than to tend his own soul. But what did that tending of the soul consist of? Not purification, as the ancient religious cults had advocated, and certainly not belief in things unseen and unproved. It consisted of cultivation of rational knowledge, of adherence to a course of life, not because one blindly believes some teaching, but because one (in the strongest sense) knows what is truly good. Nor can one find anywhere in Plato any equating of the great and the small, or any suggestion that the foolish are as good as the wise. On the contrary, only knowledge, which is the possession of the few who are truly blessed, is entitled to govern either the individual or the state. And where Aristotle upheld the cultivation of wisdom and the rational life as the ultimate ideal of human nature (as that ideal which quite literally, he thought, most closely approached the divine), the early Christians, on the contrary, taught that it was the life of faith that would lead us to salvation; a faith that was in little need of real knowledge and even less need of reason. Indeed, given this faith, this total belief in what was not and could not ever be known at all, even the most simple and ignorant could hope to share in the divine.

THE CORRUPTION OF GOODNESS

When one contemplates the confrontation of the Christian religion with the pagan ideals of antiquity, it seems almost as if some malevolent and supernatural genius, some "evil demon" in Descartes's apt expression, had considered all the basic presuppositions and ideals of the great moralists of antiquity and then, one by one, craftily devised the very *opposite* in an effort to corrupt them. Then, aware that these opposites could never survive the light of reason and wisdom on which the ancient ethical ideals rested, this genius had declared reason and worldly wisdom themselves to be obstacles to enlightenment, substituting a kind of blindness or faith in their place, and exhorting all to trust in its guidance. Some such graphic contrast is, in any case, needed in order to see that the moral ideals of Christianity have not always seemed worthy of consideration, and that they are, in fact, in diametrical opposition to a wisdom that is timeless and that really rests upon only one presupposition. This presupposition is that human beings—or at least some of them—among all creatures have the unique capacity for the exercise of intelligence and reason. It never occurred to the ancient moralists that the perfection of human nature could be hoped for through any other pursuit. And above all it never occurred to them that the least among human beings could, in the eyes of the gods or by any other standard, be as *good,* that is, as virtuous or excellent as the best. One can declare today that the least significant person, someone utterly lacking in wisdom or knowledge, might nevertheless be every bit as virtuous as the wise and not be greeted with laughter. To the ancients that would have seemed unintelligible at best and a contradiction at worst. That is because the meaning of *virtue* has completely changed. The change was wrought by religion. It still persists, even in the minds of those who are not religious. Even they must make an effort in order to understand what Aristotle, for example, meant by "a good man." No contemporary of Aristotle's would have failed to understand. Indeed, no Athenian would have misunderstood, prior to the advent of Christianity.

THE DIVERGENT PATHS OF ETHICS AND SCIENCE

Physical science and medicine, growing upon the rational foundations laid down by the Greeks, have flourished and now stand as an awesome tribute not only to the ideal of rational thought and inquiry, which their culture gave us, but to their overwhelming power. To understand the baneful state of ethics in contrast to this, one might imagine the following. Suppose that, in the early stages of the development of medicine, a cult had arisen to proclaim that the true ideals and methods of medicine are really quite the opposite of those that have prevailed among the ancients; that, for example, true health is characterized by debility, fever, and pain; that the best therapies, therefore, consist of exposure to filth and other noxious substances, some of these being concocted according to the esoteric formulae found in books of unknown origin, and that adherence to such formulae, rather than observation and experiment, are the proper means to the disclosure of truth in this area. Surely one would be entitled to say that this would not have been the perfection of medicine but its corruption, that the science itself had been turned upside down—everything proper to it being excluded, and everything to which it should be opposed being incorporated into it.

The historical development of moral philosophy has not been entirely unlike that. Today moralists can actually declare that the weak and the stupid are, from the standpoint of morality, just as deserving as the strong and the wise; that true virtue, once understood as individual excellence, is instead the precise opposite of this, so that the least gifted of persons can, nevertheless, claim an equality with the best; and that reason, which is the unique possession of human beings is, in spite of that, of no particular moral significance, since morality is located in a certain kind of intention or will, namely, one that is benevolent and utterly unthreatening. Even a philosopher, whom one thinks of as the natural heir to the ideals of the Greeks, can with a perfectly straight face declare that pride is really no virtue, that no one is or can ever hope to be of more worth than others from the standpoint of ethics, and that, therefore, a sense of superior individual worth on the part of any person can have no moral justification. That such things can be said by persons speaking out of religious faith is not surprising, but that they can be said by philosophers is, in the light of our philosophical heritage, almost incredible. It is as though Aristotle should have pointed to his slaves and declared each and every one of them to be as good as himself! Today we can actually imagine this sort of thing and even feel an inclination to praise it—but that is because we have lost the original meaning of the word *good*, as applied to persons.

chapter 14

The Religious Framework of Modern Ethics

The corruption of philosophical ethics by religion did not consist merely of the substitution of vulgar for noble ideals. It was more thoroughly undermined by a process more insidious and so subtle that even contemporary practitioners of philosophical ethics are, for the most part, quite unaware of it.

That process consisted, as we have noted, of two things working together. The first was the absorption by philosophy of an idea quite foreign to the Greeks, but sufficiently like other concepts of ancient ethics to make the absorption fairly easy. The idea alluded to is, of course, that of moral right and wrong. And the second part of the process was the rejection of the context which gave that idea meaning, namely, that of divine command.

THE RELIGIOUS BASIS OF MORAL DISTINCTIONS

The Greeks, as we have seen, understood, as all civilized people do, the basic distinction between right and wrong. But while they did not doubt the importance of that distinction, they did not consider it to be of much significance to ethics, being an essentially practical distinction created by custom and law. However as we have also seen, religion introduced the idea of right and wrong at a higher level than that resulting from human custom and law, namely, one resulting from divine law. Modern philosophy thenceforth *kept* the distinction between moral right and wrong, making it the pivotal idea of moral philosophy, but *cast aside* the context that gave it meaning, namely God's will.

That something so astonishing could actually happen, without every thinker being acutely aware of what was happening, is partly explained by the obvious fact that the ordinary distinction between right and wrong—namely, that created by custom and law—is perfectly familiar to everyone. The illusion was thus created that the higher distinction of *moral* right and wrong must be similarly familiar, even with no assistance from religion. In fact, though, discourse on moral right and wrong, in the absence of any reference to divine law, became entirely empty and meaningless. Philosophers *thought* they were discoursing meaningfully because the bare concepts of right and wrong are certainly not without meaning to anyone. They did not notice that the extra qualification, *moral,* which gave these words a connotation quite different from anything contained in their original meaning, required more for its justification than mere familiarity. And they had rejected the very thing that gave it that justification. To say that something is wrong in the sense of being forbidden by custom is perfectly understandable but philosophically not very interesting. And to say that something is wrong because, while permitted by custom, it is forbidden by God, is also perfectly understandable to anyone who believes in a law-giving God. But to say that something is wrong, even though permitted by custom and law and, even though no God exists to forbid it, is *not* understandable—unless, of course, one considers his own abhorrence of something a reason for describing it as morally wrong. There are, to be sure, persons who rest their "moral judgments" on nothing more substantial than such feelings, but no philosophy can turn on that sad fact.

THE SEARCH FOR A PHILOSOPHICAL BASIS OF MORAL LAW

Alternatively, one can try to find some source of law other than God and yet higher and more authoritative than any human will. And philosophers have tried this—have tried, in other words, to find some law or principle of ethics that would give meaning to this higher sense of right and wrong, without resorting to the idea of any law of God. But it has never succeeded. This should be apparent to anyone who reads any modern philosophical moralist. One finds the discourse larded with such words as "right," "dutiful," "just," and so on. The impression given is that such ethical terms are not to be understood in their merely conventional sense, as expressing only customary permissions and prohibitions more or less idiosyncratic to the philosopher's own culture. And yet, failing to cite any source of them higher than custom, they are left with no clear meaning at all. The reader has a kind of illusion of understanding but really no understanding at all; and philosophers, because they are able to discourse in such terms with consistency and often with much subtlety, are caught up in precisely the same illusion, which is, in their case, almost impossible to expose.

Two examples from modern philosophy will illustrate that point. The examples are the moral philosophies of Immanuel Kant and John Stuart Mill. They are chosen because they are often represented as diametrically opposed to each other, which in some ways they are. But with respect to the point we are making, they are in total agreement. Each tries to give content to the distinction between moral right and wrong, without recourse to any divine lawgiver. They try to base this distinction on reason or experience, not faith. Each formulates a law from which that distinction is supposed to follow. But the source of that law is neither custom nor any human legislator, for if it were, the distinction of right and wrong would be merely conventional and relative, and without moral authority. Nor, as noted, is God the source. For Kant the source is reason and for Mill, experience.

KANT'S SEARCH FOR A SUPREME LAW OF ETHICS

There is no need to render a comprehensive account of Kantian ethics in order to make the points just alluded to. We need only to look at the foundations of his ethics, which he, significantly, called "metaphysical."

Kant regarded it as too obvious for argument that the distinction of right and wrong or, more particularly in his philosophy, the concept of duty is derivative from the concept of law. Duty is even defined as respect for law. Law, in turn, is quite rightly defined by him as a kind of command or, as he preferred, an "imperative," which means exactly the same thing. Moral duty cannot result from the command of any king or other human legislator, however, for such a command can be no more than the expression of the will of one human being, however exalted he may be. The will expressed in the command of one human being can quite properly be rejected in the will of another. One person can sometimes properly claim *political* authority over another, but no person can claim *moral* authority over another. The authority of the command must, therefore, be such as to be binding on every human will and not merely on those who happen to be subject to this or that human legislator.

Of course, any commandment of God possesses that authority, but Kant, proposing to rest his metaphysical ethics on reason rather than faith, cannot turn to God for the needed authority. To what authority, then, does he turn? To that of some venerable philosopher or sage? No, for such a person, however wise, is still merely human. Then to what? To reason itself. Human reason, Kant supposes, does not invent and proclaim, but *engenders* a law or imperative that it recognizes as universally binding on rational beings. It is, unlike other commands, not the expression of any will, human or divine, nor unlike the customs and laws of societies does it have any purely practical justification. It expresses an absolute, or uniquely moral, obligation or duty merely for the sake of that duty itself and is for this reason called *categorical*. So act, this categorical imperative says, that you could will the maxim of your action to be a universal law, binding on all rational beings. This same categorical imperative is otherwise expressed as a command to treat rational nature always as an end, never as a means. And while the two formulations seem different in meaning, they are claimed by Kant to be identical in the one thing that matters: they are commands that express, not the will of any man or God, but the reason of every rational being. This command does not bid one to so act because thus commanded by any legislator, priest, or wise philosopher. It does not bid one to act in such a manner that human existence may be made better or societies flourish, for that is the role of customs and laws, which yield only conventional ethics. It bids one to so act simply because that is the essence of duty, or in other words, because that is the nature of *moral* obligation as distinguished from all obligations that are merely human.

Reason, accordingly, is invoked to fill what had hitherto been the role of God with respect to moral right and wrong: to command, and thereby create a law and a concept of duty, transcending the laws and duties that, however important, are of merely human fabrication.

But of course the difficulty with that is that reason discovers no such command, nor would even the most sagacious of philosophers ever have suspected the existence of such a law had Kant never lived to invent it. The idea of a command in the absence of any commander is inherently absurd, as is the idea of an obligation or duty which is not a duty to any person or persons, or to any *polis* or state, or to any gods. An obligation is inherently an obligation *to* some person or group, divine or human, and can no more stand by itself, without relationship to any such being, than can, say, the idea of being a descendant, or spouse, or having a debt. All such ideas express relationships, and so does the idea of obligation. Representing such obligation as moral, in order to convey that it is higher than one's obligation to any Caesar or king, does not suddenly eliminate the need for it to be an obligation to *some* person or group. It was once thought of as the obligation to heed the commands of God. But if God is removed from consideration, as Kant insists, then the concept of obligation or duty is left suspended in thin air, devoid of any meaning at all. That it still *seems* meaningful to Kant and his followers results only from the fact that, even in the absence of God, we still feel the need for such an idea, which was originally the offspring of religion. And that such a law is described as discoverable by reason—even, Kant says, by the untutored reason of a peasant—attests only to the philosopher's perfectly proper veneration of reason as distinct from faith. *Something* was needed to give authority to this presumed law, something higher than human will or desire, but something nevertheless natural, and not supernatural. What better candidate, then, than reason. Reason here steps in, to fill for the philosopher the role that had hitherto been filled by God, for the faithful. But the difficulty remains, that reason is utterly unsuited to such a role. The ancients, who glorified reason and certainly understood its transcendent importance, did not assign it the task of giving to the world moral laws of the kind envisaged by Kant, and no one since has been able to show, even to the most rational of doubters, that any such law of morality exists.

THE PRINCIPLES OF MILL'S ETHICS

J. S. Mill, following a somewhat different tradition, turned to experience rather than abstract reason in his hope of discovering some supreme principle of morality, one that would, like Kant's, or like the commands of God, be binding on all people. It was Mill's presupposition that if he could but find some one thing that is, just considered in its own nature and independently of its effects, uniquely and universally good, then he could derive his moral law from that. The law would be a command to increase that one thing that is uniquely good and, as a corollary, to minimize its opposite, which must be uniquely and universally bad.

He thought he had found that unique goodness in *pleasure* or, in what he strangely took to be the same thing, happiness. Pain was taken by him to be uniquely and universally bad, just in itself, and independently of any bad consequences that might flow from it. Therefore, he declared, our *duty* must be to increase the amount of pleasure in the world and minimize the amount of pain.

This formula, with many modifications and qualifications, has attracted a great deal of attention in philosophy, with many defenders of one version or another and many critics. One can, to be sure, doubt whether its fundamental supposition is correct, or is even suggested by our actual experience—namely, that only *one thing* is good in itself, independent of its consequences; or that only *one thing* is, with similar qualifications, inherently bad. One wonders, too, how happiness can be declared to be one and the same thing as pleasure. Surely this is not the concept of happiness (*eudaemonia*) that the ancients discoursed upon profoundly and at length.

But we can disregard all that here. What is important, for our purposes, is that Mill has failed, as conspicuously as Kant, to provide any law of duty at all and hence to give any meaning at all to moral right and wrong. One can even concede, for argument, Mill's presupposition that pleasure is always good. One can concede that it is good in itself, independent of its consequences. One can, in short, let Mill have every single claim he makes about the nature and value of pleasure and can even let him identify it with happiness, if he wishes. It still does not follow that anyone has the least moral obligation to increase it. To say that we are so obligated is simply to make a groundless assertion.

Philosophers, testing Mill's principle of duty, have argued whether, for example, one is morally obligated to lie in circumstances where a lie will produce more pleasure than the truth; or, similarly, whether one might be morally obligated to commit injustices—for example, to punish innocent persons—under those baneful conditions sometimes arising, where such a course would seem to produce less pain than adhering to the path of justice.

Such arguments raise a serious question, but they still do not touch upon the basic issue; and that is, that not only can it be questioned whether moral obligations such as these can arise, but rather that Mill's formula, in fact, yields no moral obligation whatsoever. No law of morality follows from any observation, however correct, as to what is good. That something is good, perhaps overwhelmingly and uniquely good, is sometimes a practical reason for pursuing it. Thus to describe some course of action as a path to happiness is certainly to recommend that course of action. But noting, however correctly, that such an action will, more than any other, enhance the happiness of *others,* while this may (or may not) evoke some incentive to do it, certainly imposes no obligation whatsoever to do it. To say that it does is simply to make a groundless assertion. No reason can be given for such a claim, for none exists. That something is good is one kind of claim. That this or that person is morally obligated to pursue a given course of conduct is a different kind of claim, and there is no rational connection between any two such claims no matter what their content might be.

One can perhaps best see this with an example. Let us imagine the fairly familiar kind of situation in which people are exhorted to donate small amounts of their blood, which will then be used therapeutically in hospitals. And let us make the normal suppositions about this: that such donations of blood are, with the usual safeguards, harmless to the donors and immensely beneficial to the recipients who are normally unknown to the donors. And we can suppose that, on some occasion, such donation of blood would be the best course of action that a given individual could take, in terms of the happiness of everyone concerned, most obviously the happiness of the ultimate recipients of that blood. Here we can certainly say many things: that there are reasons why the person in question might wish to be a donor; that it would be moderately generous of him to do so; that most persons who have a regard for the sick are quite willing to do this; that someday he may be in need of such a donor himself, and so on. But what *cannot* be claimed is that this individual has a *moral obligation* to donate blood because it in no way follows from any of these suggestions. He does not. If he has promised to, then he has an obligation, for he has then obligated himself to whomever he made such a promise. If he has accepted payment in return for such a service, then he is obligated to whomever has paid him. And if the laws of the state should happen to require such action, then he has a legal obligation. But in the absence of any obligations of these familiar kinds, he does *not* have any obligation here. The "moral law" that declares that he does is no law at all but only a fabrication of philosophy. No legislator, human or divine, enunciates such a law, nor does reason discover it. The only thing that is "discovered" is that something is good, and that some course of action would lead to that good. But from two such suppositions, even when they happen to be correct, nothing whatever follows concerning anyone's moral obligation.

MILL AND THE HEDONISM OF THE ANCIENTS

Mill's moral philosophy is instructive in illustrating, as well as anything can, one of the fundamental points that it has been our purpose to make, namely, that the whole enterprise of philosophical ethics was drastically altered by its absorption from religion of the ideas of moral right and wrong.

The pagan moralists of antiquity, who based their philosophies on the supposition that pleasure is uniquely and invariably good, did not try to derive from that any laws of morality or use it to distinguish right from wrong. It could never have occurred to them to do this, and that is instructive. They presupposed a common knowledge of right and wrong, that is, of the principles of justice, among those of their culture. Instead, then, of going in that direction, they addressed themselves to the question of how pleasure, that is to say a pleasant life, can be achieved. They were, in other words, concerned to know what is good, in order that they could themselves be fulfilled in it and teach others to find it as well. This is, for example, the nature of Epicurus' teaching. His philosophy is a vast collection of wise and thoughtful observations and anecdotes bearing on the ingredients of a happy existence and the means to its attainment. Not only was he unconcerned about moral duty, as we understand it, he was not even concerned with social duty, or the kind of obligations imposed by custom and tradition, except insofar as consideration of these had a bearing upon the main objective, which was a happy life.

Accordingly if we now read the Epicurean philosophy, or in fact any of the discussions of pleasure found in the ancient hedonists, we are likely to wonder why they are called *moralists,* or why their writings are categorized as *ethics.* They seem to have nothing to say about morality or ethics as we have come to understand those terms. But the reason for that should now be quite clear: Religion, representing God as a lawgiver, bequeathed to philosophy a conception of ethics based upon duty, quite unknown to the ancients. Epicurus and the other moralists of antiquity had no belief in the gods as supreme lawgivers. To them morality was nothing more than the customary practices of civilized people, which they referred to, not as morality, but as justice. Justice is, to be sure, important in the Epicurean philosophy but only because it is considered an essential ingredient of personal happiness.

Mill's philosophy, starting from the same presuppositions concerning what is good, goes in an entirely different direction. Having propounded the ideal of the greatest happiness for the greatest number, he does not devote his treatise to a consideration of just how that goal is to be achieved. He does not lay down practical guides to social and political life, all aimed at the widest distribution of happiness. Somewhat astonishingly, he says virtually nothing about the path to happiness but concentrates instead on pointing the way to distinguishing what is morally right! Why? Because the direction of moral philosophy itself had changed since its perfection by the ancients, and the change was wrought by religion. No longer did philosophy take for granted that the distinctions of justice are created by the practical rules of human custom and law. Religion had introduced a new idea of a higher law and with it a higher conception of right and wrong, eventually to evolve into the idea of moral right and wrong. Of course, that idea of a higher law made perfectly good sense so long as it was accompanied by the idea of a higher lawgiver, namely God. And it was Mill's aim, as it was Kant's, somehow to retain that idea of moral right and wrong, together with the requisite higher law, but to do this *without* appealing to any higher lawmaker. Mill thought he could do it with the idea of an ultimate good discovered in experience, just as Kant thought he could do it with the idea of a universal law discovered by reason. Neither of them succeeded. Reason discovers no moral law, and the concept of pleasure or happiness likewise implies none. Thus, it would seem, the laws that give rise to the ideas of moral right and wrong are, after all, the laws of God. Or, in case there is no law-giving God, then we should conclude that the requisite moral laws do not exist either. The religious will of course prefer the first alternative; but philosophy, if its wisdom is to rest upon reason rather than faith, must take the second. That does not mean, of course, that philosophy must abandon ethics, but only that philosophy should abandon what has been its futile search for principles for distinguishing moral right and wrong.

THE GOAL OF ETHICS

There do remain, however, the original goals of moral philosophy, among them the search for an understanding of human excellence and the nature of happiness. There remains, in other words, the ethics of aspiration. Philosophers once sought these things, and the result was a philosophical literature of inestimable value, now largely unappreciated and misunderstood because of the distorting influence of later ideas. Moral philosophy has in the meantime deteriorated into quibbles and disputes on which nothing of significance turns; usually, in the final analysis, these reduce to questions of what is really "right" and what is really "wrong," and how these things are to be known, as if, indeed, there were a possibility of understanding what such terms even mean.

chapter 15

The Virtue of Pride

It would be appropriate now to embark upon the long path, with its many bypaths, to which all the foregoing discussion points; that is, to describe the nature of human happiness, the qualities of excellence or virtue, and the ideal of human nature to which persons of a philosophical mind might aspire. We cannot do all that here, for the task is simply too large. It does need to be done, however, and the foundation for ethics of this character assuredly exists. The foundation is the rich treasure of moral philosophy created by the ancients and culminating, for them, in the ethics of Aristotle. It is a foundation upon which a great deal can be built by philosophers now living and others not yet born. Of course this should have been undertaken long ago, but philosophy in the meantime got sidetracked onto another path, that of the ethics of duty, a path which seems to have culminated in darkness. That word "darkness" is a good one to describe the proprietary haggling over words and concepts which characterizes contemporary philosophical ethics. Indeed it is worse than this, for the words around which controversy turns are for the most part jargon terms never heard outside the discourse of philosophers, having been coined by them, most of them ending with "ISM"—objectivism, emotivism, deontologism, intuitionism, rule utilitarianism, to name a few. Such is the sad state of contemporary ethics, to oppose rival theories to each other, these being not rival descriptions of virtue and happiness nor even, to a very large extent, theories of right and wrong, but rather theories of *how* the distinction between moral right and wrong is to be "known" in the first place! They are, in other words, arid epistemological disputes, wherein a subject matter is simply assumed, however groundlessly, to exist. An ethics of duty is just presupposed, as though no philosopher had ever written of happiness and the virtues. Aspiration is almost never discussed.

Of course any ethics of aspiration must withstand the criticism that its claims cannot be proved and that, therefore, rival claims from different points of view must contend with each other without any clear means of resolving them. That criticism is hardly appropriate from contemporary practitioners of philosophical ethics, however, for not a single claim made in that area has ever been shown to be true, nor could one find any area of thought where disagreement is so complete. Even the basic presuppositions and starting points are not agreed upon; indeed worse, dispute rages over how any such starting point *could* be agreed upon, philosophers dividing themselves up into the various esoteric "isms" over just that question.

Quite apart from questions of proof or knowledge, however, there remains the goal of wisdom. And only a vulgarian could suggest that no wisdom could possibly result from reflection on, say, the nature of happiness, or of friendship, or the nature and value of courage, or of personal integrity, of the kind so often alluded to by Socrates, or any of the numberless themes that occupied the thought of the classical pagan moralists. Here, in what we have been calling the ethics of aspiration, schools of philosophy might arise again and contend with each other, not to refute but to exhibit deeper wisdom and profundity and, as in antiquity, to vie for followers.

PRIDE AS A VIRTUE

We shall now illustrate, in a limited way, what we have called the ethics of aspiration, using *pride* as the example. We could consider different and doubtless more significant virtues, but this one is particularly appropriate because it is so neglected. In fact we have, for about two thousand years, been taught not even to regard it as a virtue, except perhaps in a very limited way. Pride is quite correctly perceived to be incompatible with the egalitarianism that we are so constantly admonished to uphold, as well as with the supposed virtue of humility that is so congenial to the devout mind and so foreign to the pagan temperament.

THE NATURE OF PRIDE

Pride is not a matter of manners or demeanor. One does not become proud simply by affecting certain behavior or projecting an impression that has been formed in the mind. It is a personal excellence much deeper than this.

In fact it is the summation of most of the other virtues, since it presupposes them.

Pride is the justified love for oneself. The qualification "justified" is crucial. Simpletons can love themselves and are, in fact, very apt to do so; but they are not proud, for there are no qualities of excellence to justify that love. They have not pride but mere conceit, which is something different altogether. Conceit is the simpleton's unwarranted sense of self-importance. Conceited persons thus imagine themselves as possessed of great worth, when in fact they have little or none; and that is why they are simple, as well as being very tiresome to others and of little worth in the eyes of those who are genuinely proud.

Genuinely proud people perceive themselves as better than others, and their pride is justified because their perception is correct. Thus they love themselves, not as children and ordinary people do, for these do not possess the kind of worth that justifies such self-esteem, but because they really are, in the classical sense of the term, good. Their virtues are not assimilated ones, nor do they consist merely in the kind of innocence that wins the approbation of others. Instead, they are their own in the truest sense: that they come from within themselves and win the approbation of the only judge who counts—oneself.

ARROGANCE, VANITY, AND EGOISM

Pride is not arrogance, and a proud person would never be overbearing towards others. While conceit is an attitude towards oneself, which in that respect resembles pride, arrogance is a way of behaving, a mannerism, and one that is profoundly offensive. One is arrogant only towards other persons. Arrogance cannot be exhibited in solitude, although conceit can—in vainglorious fantasy, for example, or at the other extreme, in solitary weeping.

Arrogance implies a belittling of the opinions, conduct, or personal qualities of another person in an effort to draw attention to one's own presumed superiority. It is, therefore, most easily exhibited towards persons who stand in an inferior position, such as waiters or other servants, employees, clerks, and so on. Police officers, particularly those who are vulgar or otherwise lacking in personal excellence, are very prone to arrogance, for one's inferior position cannot be more manifest than in the presence of a police officer's gun. It is for this same reason that cowards, given suitable circumstances, are likely to be arrogant. Since the fault that cancels their personal worth, namely cowardice, is so grave and ineradicable, they attempt to compensate with arrogance and browbeating or, given the opportunity, outright cruelty.

Vanity and egoism, too, must be distinguished from pride, for they have little in common with it. Vanity is the delight people derive from praise or flattering allusions to themselves, from whatever source, and with respect to whatever things are alluded to, whether significant or not. Thus vain people delight in flattering comment from inferior persons, such as from children, or even from total strangers, whereas a truly proud person would be quite oblivious to this. Vain people can even be seen trying to elicit attention and admiring comment in public places, and from persons entirely unknown to them, by their loud and excessive laughter, for example, or their swaggering gait, or by their attire, or by the importance or beauty of their companions. Thus a man sometimes enjoys entering a restaurant with a beautiful companion on his arm, even though he may never have been there before and may know no one in the room. Similarly, a woman is sometimes pleased to draw looks, even from strangers, to her tasteful clothing. Such are familiar examples of vanity, and they could be multiplied at length. It is something to which every normal person is prone, for who can fail to be pleasantly aware of the admiring attention of others? A vain person, however, seeks that attention, sometimes going to great length to get it, while a proud person tries to ignore it, and would be ashamed to actually set about trying to elicit it. This would be especially true with respect to such things as clothing, or the influence one has over other people or external things, in other words, things having no connection with one's true nature or excellence.

Egoism is similar to vanity, though perhaps some distinctions between the two are useful. Egoism is a certain cast of mind, characterized by excessive absorption in oneself, to the extent that one's awareness of others is clouded. Vanity, as noted, is the delight evoked by the favorable attention of others, quite regardless of what qualities elicit such attention. Thus egoism may be more characteristic of men, and vanity of women, though of course such broad generalizations are not without many exceptions. Men do often tend to be absorbed in themselves to the detriment of their awareness of others, seeing these others as instruments to the pursuit of their own goals. This is perhaps an expression of the male concern for power and influence. Women, on the other hand, are sometimes more concerned to be "attractive," something which has very much to do with appearance. And the lesser self-absorption on the part of women may explain, to some extent at least, their sometimes greater awareness of the feelings of others; these others might include children and animals, and this awareness sometimes rises to genuine compassion. To be sure, men are also capable of this, but there seem to be differences of degree.

Neither vanity nor egoism is very compatible with genuine pride, even though no one can hope or pretend to be entirely without them. While vain people delight in others' admiration for things they *have*—possessions, for instance—proud people have little interest in the admiration of others except for what they *are*; and even that admiration must come only from such persons, always relatively few, who are themselves proud people, in the truest sense, and hence better. Thus, while no one would want to be poor, a proud person does not mind being erroneously thought to be poor. A person of excessive vanity or egoism, on the other hand, tries very hard to create the impression of affluence even when that is a false impression, something a proud person would not think of doing. Vain or self-centered persons live beyond their means, or spend what limited resources they have on things that will be seen by others—cars, house furnishings, clothing, and so on. Such persons thus try to compensate for their limitations as persons by augmenting those things that are external to themselves and their characters. One who is quite stupid, for example, tries to compensate with a showy car or house; or one who fears danger or dreads death tries to compensate with excessive but insincere affability. They try, in other words, to be *thought* good, in the original, nonmoral sense of that term, when in fact they are not.

PRIDE AND SELF-APPROBATION

Proud people are not much concerned with what others think of them and care nothing at all for the opinions of insignificant persons, but are instead concerned with what they think of themselves. Others know you for what you appear to be, which can be misleading, but you know yourself for what you are—at least, you are in a privileged position to. If it is you who are ignorant, or silly, or weak-willed, or fearful, or vain, then, however well you may succeed in concealing these faults from others, you cannot entirely conceal them from yourself unless you are very stupid. And for this reason proud people would not try to conceal themselves from themselves nor have any reason to, regardless of how little they care about the opinions of others. For proud people, as noted, are those who *justifiably* love themselves, that is, who have a high *and correct* opinion of their real worth. They therefore do not compare themselves with others with respect to things that are extraneous to themselves. For example, they do not compare their possessions with those of their neighbors or associates, or if they happen to be aware that what they own far exceeds what their neighbors own, they do not let on to this. Instead, they compare themselves only with the best. They are properly ashamed if others are wiser than they, or if others conduct their lives with better order and rationality, or if others have greater courage and self-discipline. Similarly, their envy is reserved, not for those who are praised by the multitude, for whatever reason, but for those whose honor is deserved and is bestowed only by the best.

Proud people do not bow to any others, except in such purely ceremonious ways as tipping their hats; nor are they deferential to persons of special status or rank, such as those holding high offices, or persons who are wealthy, or persons of a special and conspicuous class, such as priests—with the exception, once again, of purely ceremonious gestures of deference, such as the use of "sir" and "ma'm" in addressing them. The most conspicuous exception to these generalizations is old people who have grown wise with their years. Such persons are truly venerable, and pride is never compromised by treating them as such. The experience of years, quite by itself, may confer wisdom, and nothing is more deserving of honor than this; so it is not inappropriate that others, aspiring to wisdom, should bow to those who have won it.

THE MARKS OF PRIDE

Pride is seen in things both great and small. One of the great tests, for example, is the individual's response to acute danger, or his or her reaction to a life-threatening disease or to humiliation at the hands of enemies. One type of person bears these things with a natural, unpracticed fortitude and nobility while, at the other extreme, some collapse into whimpering and self-pity. With respect to death, a proud person knows that even his or her own life is not worth clinging to at the cost of pride or honor; would never want it prolonged beyond the point where the virtues upon which pride rests have become debilitated; and would, for this reason, prefer to die ten years too soon than ten days too late.

And there are other great tests, such as one's reaction to the death of a son or daughter who was intelligent, and strong, and filled with promise of great achievement.

But such things as these are negative, being tests of strength in adversity. There are great positive tests as well: the power one displays in writing and speech, sensitivity to music and other things of great beauty, and perhaps above all else, one's own creative power. Whether you follow experience and reason to form your beliefs on either great or petty matters, or whether, on the other hand, you simply embrace whatever opinions answer to your fondest desires, this, as well as any other test, distinguishes a wise and proud person from a vain and foolish one. Thus people who are given to ideologies and faiths, that is, to large and untested claims that they find satisfying and reassuring, are not wise and cannot therefore be proud; for whatever love they may have for themselves can hardly be justified. On the other hand, those who accept even unpleasant facts because they are facts, or do not shrink from drawing appropriate inferences from what they observe, even when these facts or observations may run counter to everything they have been taught and everything they desperately hope is true, such persons are wise, whether learned or not, and have at least that one correct basis for self-approbation. If, in addition, they are learned, then they have still another. And if, in addition to those qualities, they are creative, self-disciplined, and courageous, then they have still others; and there comes a point where external things which contribute nothing to those qualities are clearly seen by them to be worth very little, however much they may delight simple people.

But there are also, as noted, lesser marks of pride, easily recognized by other proud persons, though not understood by the meek and the foolish. A proud person is, for example, serious, but not solemn, whereas a meek person's effort to be serious results only in a laughable solemnity. Such a person puts on a grave face and a reserved manner and imagines that he or she has become serious. Hearty laughter and the enjoyment of life are compatible with seriousness, which is positive and affirmative, but not with mere solemnity, which is negative and withdrawn. Again, a proud person is not garrulous and does not speak merely for the sake of "making conversation" or of hearing words flow. On matters not worthy of comment—such as weather, minor political issues, or things in the immediate surroundings— proud people normally say nothing at all. They do not mind long periods of dead silence, feel no embarrassment or anxiety at this, nor any need to break such silence with idle observations except when silence would be interpreted as rudeness. Proud people delight in the company of other proud and worthwhile persons, and seek above all to discover and appreciate their strengths and virtues. Their awareness of these is not clouded by self-absorption, nor by any desire to project a good impression of themselves; for they know that their own excellences will be recognized by others of similar excellence and do not care if they are not seen by those who lack this.

One category of behavior which is sometimes erroneously associated with pride is the fastidious observance of what is called etiquette. Etiquette comprises the many rules of social intercourse, often petty in nature, which enable people to associate comfortably in special circumstances such as social gatherings. These rules are often important in preventing embarrassment and awkwardness, but they have almost nothing to do with pride and can sometimes even work against it. Thus, proud people are not ashamed to whistle in public places where such behavior is harmless though uncommon, nor do they mind wearing old or baggy clothing, for example, if that is their taste. Etiquette, by its very nature, encourages a kind of mindless conformity, whereas those who are proud conform their behavior to standards which are their own.

A proud person does not pretend to an insincere equality with others who are inferior, that is, who are meek, foolish, or silly. A person is not worthy of esteem just by the fact of being a person but, rather, by the fact of being a person of outstanding worth, which is something quite rare.

THE PLACE OF EXTERNALS

Among the lesser marks of pride are also those things that moralists once referred to as "externals," meaning by this all those things that are extraneous to what a person inherently is. Dress, for instance, is an external thing, as are one's reputation and standing in the popular mind, the praise or honors one receives from small-minded people, and so on.

Thus, with respect to dress, proud people do not ask what others expect of them, or how they wish them to look, and the least consideration in their minds is how *others* dress. They ask instead what will please themselves. It is compatible with perfect and beautiful pride never to wear a suit or necktie, to dress in baggy trousers and sweat shirt and cheap shoes. This description fits the appearance of one of the proudest persons of our century, Albert Einstein, whose almost superhuman virtues were combined with a boundless compassion and sweetness. But let it be added that affectation in dress, or the deliberate attempt to be outlandish and to attract the attention of others, is not pride but, as noted before, vanity. For again, the good opinion that one should seek is one's own, not others', and certainly not that of strangers.

PRIDE AND MORALITY

With respect to what is popularly called "morality," a proud person is in the best sense the creator of his or her own. Nothing is done *merely* because it is recommended and done by others. Rather, something is done because *he* or *she* sees it as worthy of being done, and especially because it is worthy of himself or herself. Thus a proud person would not injure or betray a friend, not because it would be "wrong," or would violate vulgar morality, but because it would be shameful. Nor would a proud person cheat or take dishonest advantage of anyone, again, not because it would be wrong, but because it would be incompatible with his or her own worth. To act otherwise would imply that there are external things that are of greater importance than one's own excellence, which would be totally inconsistent with pride. But perhaps the clearest indication of the ethics of pride is found in those situations for which popular morality has no clear rules. Consider, for example, the finding of things whose ownership is uncertain, or for which no owner can be determined at all. Thus, for example, if money or other valuables are found on the ground, a proud person does not hesitate to take them; but such a person could not be imagined seeing someone drop these things and then picking them up unless, of course, to restore them to the person who dropped them. The reason for such behavior does not rest upon any common notion of theft but on one's own clear notion of honor. But perhaps the best illustration of all is found in the opportunity to take money or other valuables from a corpse. These things, in the nature of the case, do not belong to anyone (assuming no surviving kin) and are thus, for all practical purposes, simply found. There is no clear rule of popular morality covering such a situation, for it is of rare occurrence, never occurring at all in the lives of most people. Yet a proud person would not have the slightest inclination to do such a thing, and for a reason that is overwhelming and conclusive, namely that such an act would be shameful. It is not shameful in the sense that we have been taught to regard it as such, for little has ever been said on such infrequent things. Rather, it is shameful in the true sense of the word, as being incompatible with one's own worth as a person, a worth that is possessed only by the proud. To be sure, this does leave humble persons with little incentive for personal honor, but that is not an untoward consequence, for such persons have little of this incentive anyway. They can be cajoled to decency by others, or compelled by laws and morality, but a genuinely proud person is cajoled to nothing at all by others, and is law-abiding and moral only as a condition of civilized life. Someone possessed of personal excellence requires more than morality for a life that is, in its true and original sense, good.

Such (in outline and with much omitted) is the virtue of pride. It is not the only virtue, nor even the highest, that being, without doubt, wisdom; but it is nevertheless, in the sense that was explained, a kind of summation of the virtues.

It is also a specimen of aspiration, which cannot be proved to be worth having. But in this area little can be proved anyway. We are dealing not with things that are true, in the usual sense, but with things that are good, in the philosophical sense. And as to the question whether this or any other virtue is worth having and worth giving a great deal to have, one has, of course, to find the answer within oneself. Conduct can sometimes be forced upon one, but virtue can only be discovered.

chapter 16

Happiness

Underlying all the moral philosophy of the ancients were two questions: What is happiness? And how is it attained? Those are the questions to which we now, finally, turn.

Happiness has to be the basic concern of all ethics, for if human beings had no capacity for it and for its opposite, there would be no point in reflecting about ethics at all. This was so obvious to the ancients that it seemed to them to need no defense. All these classical moralists justified their systems, finally, by claiming that the ideals they portrayed were the ingredients of a happy life. Even Plato felt the need to justify the austere lives of the guardians of his republic by claiming that they were, notwithstanding appearances, happy; and he recognized the suggestion that they were not as a possibly fatal criticism. The Stoics, too, in spite of their unbending rectitude and the severity of their principles, maintained that their ideal life of reason and self-denial was the only genuinely happy one.

The idea of happiness is no less essential to modern moral philosophy than to the ancient systems, even though it is now more apt to be taken for granted than treated as a difficult and profoundly important idea in its own right. The role of happiness in determining questions of moral right and wrong is generally acknowledged, but then attention is forthwith focused not on the nature of happiness, but upon the distinction of right and wrong.

Still, no philosopher could consider his theories tenable if he were compelled to admit that the application of them to human affairs would inevitably promote misery. Even those who reject hedonism, and the various forms of utilitarianism, would find it hard to render their views plausible if they had to assume that human beings have no more capacity for happiness than unfeeling stones. However one approaches ethics—whether from the ancient standpoint of virtue, or the modern one of duty, or from any other— what one finally asserts has to be something that makes a difference and this, in the last analysis, must be a difference with respect to human happiness. Otherwise, whatever is said will be simply pointless.

THE NATURE OF HAPPINESS

However much the ancient schools differed in their various conceptions of happiness, they were agreed about its importance. Their word for it, *eudaimonia,* is not even adequately translatable into English. It usually comes out, in translation, as "happiness," but not without loss. Something like "fulfillment" would in some ways be better, but we shall stay with happiness, keeping in mind its shortcomings.

Eudaimonia means, literally, to be possessed of a good demon, and this conveys the idea of extreme good fortune on the part of its possessor. One possessed of *eudaimonia* was thought of by the ancients as blessed beyond measure, as having won something of supreme worth and, at the same time, something very elusive and hence rare. Just what it *is* was seldom clear, even in the minds of the greatest moralists, but there was no doubt at all of its importance and value. To discover the nature of this *eudaimonia* and the path to its attainment seemed to many great moralists of that age to be the main task of philosophy.

Most people seem to think they know what happiness is, which is unfortunate, for this prevents them from learning. One has no incentive to inquire into what one thinks one already knows. In fact, however, there seem to be few things more infected with error and false notions than people's ideas of happiness. It is very common for people, in their ill-considered quest for personal happiness, to spend their lives pursuing some specious ideal— such as the accumulation of wealth—and then, having succeeded, to miss the happiness erroneously identified with it. Of course people are reluctant to come to terms with their own illusions, and few who have wasted their lives are very willing to admit it even to themselves; but their failure is often quite obvious to others. We tend to be tolerant of error here, for its only victims are the possessors of it. Another person's dashed expectations seldom threaten our own. And we are therefore content to suppose that if someone seems to himself or herself to be happy, perhaps he or she really is happy after all. But one can see how shallow this is by asking whether one would really wish to *be* that other person. It is hard to see why not, if that other person is believed to be truly happy. But we know, in fact, that such persons are not; they only seem so to themselves, largely because they are unwilling to admit their own folly.

It was from reflections such as these that ancient moralists were fond of quoting Solon, to the effect that no man should be deemed happy until he is dead (for example, Aristotle, *N. Ethics*, Bk. I, Ch. 10). This paradoxical remark seems to suggest that the dead are more happy than the living, but that is not what is meant at all. The point is, rather, that the search for happiness is the task of a lifetime and that it can elude one, even at the last moment. And indeed, it does elude most persons, even those who thought they were on the track of it.

It will be best to begin, then, by citing a few of the things that are most commonly confused with happiness and seeing where they fail. Having cleared the way of false conceptions, we can hope to see, however imperfectly, what happiness really is and how it might be won.

HAPPINESS AND PLEASURE

It is very common for modern philosophers, and others too, to confuse happiness with pleasure. John Stuart Mill even declared them to be one and the same. Others make the same mistake, sometimes speaking as if happiness were something which, like pleasures, can come and go or be artificially induced or evoked by stimulation. The ancients rarely did this. They were partly protected from this error by having a word, *eudaimonia*, far richer in its connotations than either of our words *happiness* or *pleasure*. The identification of happiness with pleasure would have sounded funny to them, whereas to us it may not.

The reason why modern philosophers are sometimes so eager to treat happiness and pleasure as the same is not hard to see. They want to think of happiness as something familiar, identifiable, and even measurable, rather than as something problematical or dubious. Pleasure, being an actual and common feeling, is certainly familiar and identifiable, and there seems to be no reason in principle why it should not be measurable. In short, the interest some moral philosophers have in the concept of pleasure is but a consequence of their predilection for empiricism. If, they think, ethics can be grounded in something plainly real and indisputable, then it ought to be possible to resolve the problems of ethics in a straightforward manner. This was certainly Mill's motive. He wanted to be able to define moral right and wrong (and hence duty) in terms of happiness and to identify happiness with pleasure, in order to remove questions of ethics from the realm of philosophical and religious polemic and to settle them beyond further controversy. And the motive of contemporary utilitarian philosophers is, at least in some cases, quite transparently similar. It has long been the hope of moral philosophers to be able to *prove* that certain things are right, certain things wrong, certain things dutiful, and it has seemed to some that basing the definitions of such normative terms on something non-normative, or factual and familiar to all, offers the best hope of being able to do that.

Familiar modes of discourse also suggest to some that pleasure and happiness might be equated. For example, being happy and being pleased seem, at one level, to be about the same. Someone who is happy with something—with his job, for instance—can also be described as pleased with it. And it is but a short step to equate being pleased with having feelings of pleasure.

Or again, it is perhaps quite impossible to imagine that someone might be happy while consistently and continuously exhibiting the symptoms of pain, or be thoroughly unhappy while continuously or repeatedly exhibiting the usual signs of pleasure. Thus do pleasure and happiness, or pain and unhappiness, seem clearly connected, not just causally, but logically. And it is not hard to suppose that the connection might be one of identity or, in other words, that happiness and pleasure might just be two words for one and the same thing.

In fact, however, happiness and pleasure have little in common other than that both are sought, and both are sometimes loosely referred to by the same vocabulary.

Pleasures, for example, can often be located in this or that part of the body. This is even more obvious in the case of pains. But one cannot speak of the happiness felt in his back when it is being massaged, or of the unhappiness in one's tooth or toe. Again, pleasures, like pains, come and go, and can be momentary; but one cannot momentarily be a happy person. One can momentarily exult or rejoice, to be sure, and while such states are typically ingredients of a happy existence, they are certainly not the same thing. Even persons who are quite plainly not happy can nevertheless feel occasional pleasures, just as those who are happy sometimes feel pain; and just as thoroughly unhappy people once in a while exult or rejoice, so do genuinely happy people sometimes feel dejection and frustration.

Again, pleasures sometimes arise from bad sources, just as pains sometimes arise from good ones; but one can hardly speak of genuine happiness as being rooted in evil or unhappiness growing from what is wholesome and good. There would, for example, be something incongruous in describing someone as achieving genuine and lasting happiness from the contemplation of suffering, though there are persons who apparently derive pleasure from such sources and from others as bad. And that reflection suggests another point of contrast, namely, that the term *happiness* is one of approbation, while pleasure is not, or at least not in the same way. Thus one can speak of happiness as an achievement, and admire those few people who manage to win it; but one hardly thinks of pleasures that way, not even those pleasures that are thought to be refined and even noble. It is at least moderately inspiring that someone, born to a wretched existence, should somehow die a happy person; but no comparable response is evoked by the thought of such a person dying with feelings of pleasure, even though this is, to be sure, preferable to its opposite. Happiness can even be thought of as the supreme good, as many philosophers have indeed described it; but it is hard to think of pleasures that way.

Furthermore, there are many different kinds of pleasures—the pleasures of eating, for instance, or of music, or of receiving praise. Pleasures are innumerable and varied. But there are not different kinds of happinesses, and indeed, even to use the word "happiness" in the plural is odd. No such oddness attaches to speaking of many pleasures. One is happy or he is not, or he is more or less so; but one cannot move from one happiness to another that is quite unlike it, as one sometimes moves from pleasure to pleasure.

And from that observation it can be noted that happiness and pleasure are really quite different kinds of things to begin with. Pleasures are, in the strictest sense, feelings, just as are pains; but happiness, and similarly unhappiness, are opposite states, not feelings. One can, to be sure, feel happy or unhappy—but not the way one feels a pleasure or pain. Feeling unhappy is feeling oneself to be in a certain general state. Pleasures and pains, on the other hand, are typically, and often quite literally, things felt—the pain of a toothache, for instance.

THE "HAPPINESS" OF LESSER BEINGS

Finally, it should be noted that children, idiots, barbarians, and even animals are perfectly capable of experiencing pleasure and pain, but none of these can become happy, in the sense in which the term is used here. One can, to be sure, speak correctly of a happy child, or a happy moron, but we need to attend carefully to what is being said in such cases. A happy child, for instance, is one who fares well *as a child,* or in other words, one for whom the benign conditions of well-being are met. These include affection, the sense of trust and security, loving discipline, and so on. Under such conditions a child can, indeed, be a *happy child,* in the sense of not being morose, disturbed, depressed, sullen, and so on, which is a perfectly clear sense of happiness. But the child is not happy in the sense that is important to philosophy, that is, in the sense of having achieved fulfillment or having been blessed with the highest personal good. This is the kind of happiness that can only be hoped for in time in the case of a child. The happiness of a happy child, though real and important, consists of little more than feeling good, a feeling that is rooted in certain salubrious conditions of life. It is a good, but it is not the great good that is the object of the moral life, the kind of good that normally takes the better part of a lifetime to attain.

The point is perhaps better made with the example of a happy moron. A person thus severely limited in those capacities that are so distinctively human can, like a child, feel happy. But that is about all his or her happiness is—a feeling. Such a person fares well, to be sure, but only as a moron, not as a person, in the full sense of the term. The point can be seen very readily if, contemplating a happy moron, one puts the matter to oneself this way: Happiness is the ultimate personal good, and this person is obviously happy. Would I not, then, be willing to be just like that moron, if I could thereby enjoy the same happiness? Of course the answer for any normal person is a resounding negative. This shows, not that happiness is not the ultimate personal good, but rather, that the happiness here illustrated is not the kind of happiness that a philosopher upholds as the highest good. Happiness, in this fuller sense, is much more than just a state of euphoria. It is the fulfillment of a person, as a person, and not as a child, or a moron, or whatever other limited person one might suggest.

PLEASURE AS AN INGREDIENT OF HAPPINESS

We can surely conclude, then, that happiness and pleasure are not the same, and that the concept of happiness, unlike that of pleasure, is a profound and difficult one.

Yet it would be rash to dismiss pleasure as having nothing to do with genuine happiness. It would be truer to say that pleasure, along with other things, is an ingredient of happiness, in the sense that no life that was utterly devoid of pleasures could ever be described as a fully happy one however estimable it might be otherwise.

Pleasure, then, should be included within that vast and heterogeneous assortment of things that the ancient moralists classed as *externals*. This apt term was applied to all those things of value to one's life, which result from accident or good fortune, or are bestowed by others. What others bestow, they can also withhold, and similarly, one can be cursed by chance as readily as one can be blessed. Externals, in short, do not depend upon oneself, are largely or entirely beyond one's own control, and are for that very reason called externals.

And it is clear that persons cannot, for the most part, bestow pleasures upon themselves. They need other things and other persons as the source of them. This does not render them bad, but it does make them largely a matter of luck. They belong in a happy life but cannot be made the whole point of it. Genuine happiness, on the other hand, while it can be utterly ruined by chance—by dreaded illness, for example, or other disaster—nevertheless depends on oneself, in case it is ever won. Wisdom, or the choice of the right path to happiness, cannot guarantee that one will win it; but on the other hand, one is certain to miss it without that wisdom.

It would thus be as narrow to identify happiness with pleasure as to identify it with any other external good, such as property, honor, youth, beauty, or whatever. External goods are goods, and while a happy life cannot be devoid of them all, neither can any sum of them, however great, add up to such a life.

HAPPINESS AND POSSESSIONS

It would be unnecessary even to consider the identification of happiness with the accumulation of wealth were it not that shallow people, who are very numerous, tend to make precisely that identification. The pursuit of happiness is simply assumed by many to be the quest for possessions, and the "good life" is thought by the same persons to be a life of affluence.

The explanation for this, too, is not hard to find. Possessions, up to a certain minimum, are essential even to life. They are needed, beyond that point, for leisure; and while life is possible without leisure, happiness is not. There is, accordingly, a natural and wise inclination in everyone to possess things. If we add to this that all persons tend to be covetous and envious, then we have most of the explanation for the widespread greed for possessions, and of the identification of happiness with the feeding of that greed. Indeed, accumulation, and the display of wealth, sometimes become important mainly as a means to inciting envy.

It should, however, be obvious to any thinking person that happiness cannot possibly be found in the sheer accumulation of possessions, even when they are used to purchase great power, or when they are philanthropically used for the public good, as sometimes happens. Such purchase of power and bestowals of wealth sometimes mitigate the ugliness of the greed lying behind them, but these cannot add up to happiness in anyone. And if happiness is the great goal in life, as it surely is, then there are obscure, unknown people, of modest possessions, far more to be envied for what they have than even the very richest.

The pursuit of possessions beyond a certain point, far from constituting or even contributing to happiness, is an obstacle to it; for one has no chance of finding the right path to anything if he is resolutely determined to follow the wrong one, convinced that he is already doing things exactly right. The feeling of power that great wealth sometimes nourishes, and the envy that is incited in others, are both exhilarating, but neither can be regarded as an important ingredient of personal happiness. At best they add zest and challenge to one's life, effectively banishing boredom, but this is a poor substitute for happiness. Indeed the lover of possessions, who indulges that love to the exclusion of things more important, can be compared to the glutton, who indulges his love for food. For food, too, is necessary for life; but gluttony, far from constituting or even contributing to a good life, is utterly incompatible with it. To set that as one's ideal of life would be grotesque, and the clearest possible example of a wasted life. The successful pursuit of great wealth is no less grotesque and as certainly the waste of one's life. Most persons who would be repelled by gluttony, however, seem strangely blind to this comparison.

And this is really sad. For each of us does, indeed, have but one life to live, and if possible that life should be lived successfully. The chance of this happening is greatly diminished when the term *success* is applied to a kind of life which, from the standpoint of philosophy, is incompatible with success. That term should be reserved for the achievement of genuine happiness, and not for some popularly accepted illusion of happiness. If, to pursue the comparison once more, there were a race of people who exalted food without limit, indulged in gluttony, and envied corpulence as the mark of success in this pursuit, then we would say with certainty that theirs was a false and in fact disgusting ideal; nor would we change our judgment of them even if they declared with one voice that this was their happiness. The illusion of happiness is not happiness, nor is the feeling of happiness always a mark of possessing it.

HONOR, FAME, AND GLORY

The same can be said of many of the other goals people set for themselves, although some of these, such as the love of honor, come closer to the ideal. A person is sometimes honored for what he actually is, and if this is something that is noble, then that honor is well placed and its recipient is, to some extent, justified in believing that he has achieved something worthwhile. Still, such things as honor, fame, and glory, though certainly not despicable, do depend upon others and must therefore be classed as externals. One can seek honor, for example, and even honor that is deserved; but whether one gets it will always depend upon the perceptions and values and, sometimes, the caprices of others. One cannot bestow honors upon oneself. People tend, moreover, to honor and applaud their own benefactors, or sometimes even people who merely make them feel very good, such as charismatic clergy and the like, rather than honoring virtue for its own sake. What they give then resembles the price of a purchase more than a gift. Thus a victorious general is honored, rather than a losing one, even though the latter might in fact have displayed more resourcefulness and courage than the former. Similarly, a person may become rich at the expense of others, then be honored for charitably returning part of it to the very public that was exploited.

Moreover, people sometimes honor and even glorify things that are neither honorable nor glorious such as sheer power, even when it is selfishly used. Also, the masses of people are often eager to raise to great fame persons whose uniqueness is some mere eccentricity; this is sometimes true of popular entertainers, or something of very little worth, as in the case of prizefighters. People can, in fact, be swept off their feet by trifles and are willing to heap great honor and wealth upon the producers of such trifles, as in the case of professional athletes, who represent no group and no ideal other than by the outright sale of their skills.

Perhaps the fairest thing to say concerning such things as we have been considering—wealth, honor, glory, and the like—is that, like pleasure, they often contribute to happiness but never add up to it. Personal excellence or even heroism are often parts of a lasting happiness, and the recognition of such qualities by others often adds to that happiness. But the real reward of personal excellence, of the kind that leads one to do, perhaps with almost superhuman effort and resourcefulness, what no one else has ever done, is simply the possession of that excellence itself. To be uniquely able to create an extraordinary piece of music of great merit, or a poem, or a story, or a philosophical treatise, or a painting, or a building, or to accomplish any feat of great significance requiring genius or exemplary courage—all such abilities are gifts in themselves that are not much embellished by the gifts added by others. What one finds satisfying are things belonging to oneself rather than things added. At the same time, it would be unrealistic to treat the recognition or acclaim of others as worth nothing. What we should say is that such honor and acclaim are sometimes a part of one's happiness, possibly even a necessary part; but they can never constitute the sum and substance of it.

EUPHORIA, JOY, AND EXUBERANCE

It is, as we have noted, common to treat happiness as if it were a mere feeling, and even to confuse it with the feelings of pleasure. But while such feelings, and particularly the feelings of joy and exuberance, are often the expressions of a real inner happiness, they are not the same. They are too fleeting and superficial, and sometimes nothing more than the expressions of mood or of momentary satisfaction. And they are rarely chosen. Happiness, on the other hand, is an essential part of one's very existence, in the case of those lucky enough to possess it. While it is not gained simply by choice, as if nothing more were required in order to have it, it is nevertheless something chosen as contrasted with something accidental or thrust upon one.

WHAT HAPPINESS IS

The idea of happiness, we have suggested, contains the idea of fulfillment. It is also something of great and perhaps even ultimate value, and except when destroyed by accident or disaster, it is enduring. It is not something that comes and goes from one hour to the next. We have also said that it is a state of being and not a mere feeling.

It can be compared with something like health, to derive a useful analogy. For while there is such a thing as the feeling of health, no one imagines that health itself is no more than a feeling. To be healthy is to be in a certain state, the description of which we will consider shortly. And like happiness, it is very precious. Again like happiness, health is something that is normally lasting; one is not momentarily healthy. Nor, like happiness, are there different kinds of health. One either possesses it or does not. And for this reason the word "health" like the word "happiness" can only be used in the singular. Health, when one has it, is usually lost only through accident or disaster not through choice; so again, the comparison with happiness is apt.

The one way in which the analogy of health to happiness breaks down significantly is with respect to choice. Health is normal and natural; one can almost say, that one is normally born with it. It is something chosen and worked for only under unusual circumstances and then only in a limited way, as in the case of someone who has lost it and strives to recover it. Happiness, on the other hand, is certainly not a gift of nature; it is quite rare and is always the fruit of choice and effort exercised over a long period of time. Effort is needed to keep or regain health but not to win it in the first place, and in this respect it is quite unlike happiness.

Still, the analogy is useful, for health, like happiness, is a kind of fulfillment. And here it is very easy to see, in a general way, just what that fulfillment consists of. One is healthy when his body and all its parts function as they should. A diseased or unhealthy body is one that functions poorly. Similarly, a diseased or unhealthy heart, or lung, or whatever, is one whose function has been partially or wholly lost, so that a diseased heart and a malfunctioning one, for example, are exactly the same thing.

HAPPINESS AND THE CONCEPT OF FUNCTION

The point of making those seemingly banal observations about health is to bring out the important point that it is understood and defined entirely in terms of *function*. And since the analogy between happiness and health appears so very close, we seem justified in supposing that happiness, too, may be understandable in terms of function.

But function of what? If health consists simply of a properly functioning body, then what is happiness? The idea of happiness is obviously larger than that of health because, although this has not been noted before, the former presupposes the latter: A person can be healthy and lack happiness but not the other way around. Someone lacking health, however courageous or otherwise estimable he or she may be, cannot be fully happy, unless one of those rare individuals who combines great inner strength with extraordinary creative power—as will be explained shortly.

And this suggests that happiness is understandable as consisting of the proper functioning of a person as a whole. With this reflection it will be seen that we have come around full circle and back to the viewpoint of the ancient moralists who defined virtue in much the same way. We see, abstractly, the plausibility of the claim they so often made, that virtue and happiness are inseparable.

Let us now look a little more closely at happiness as thus conceived and then see whether this conception of it is borne out by actual experience.

The ancients quite rightly singled out the intellectual side of human nature as constituting our uniqueness. The exercise of this was, they thought, our proper function, and excellence in this exercise our special virtue. They called this part of our nature "reason"; but this meant for them simply the exercise of intelligence in discovering truth as well as in governing conduct. Socrates and Plato construed reason more narrowly, sometimes identifying it with dialectic, that is, with philosophical argumentation. Modern philosophers have, for the most part, unfortunately gone along with this narrower conception.

Let us, then, think of reason or intelligence in a broader sense, to include not merely the activity of reasoning (as exhibited for example in philosophy) but also observation and reflection and, above all, creative activity. This is, certainly, what distinguishes us from everything else. Human beings are, by virtue of their intelligence, capable of *creating* things that are novel, unique, sometimes of great value, and even sometimes, though rarely, of overwhelming value. One thinks, for example, of scientific theories or great works of art or literature, or profound philosophical treatises like Spinoza's *Ethics,* or the great and lasting music that emerges from the creative genius of one person. It is here, certainly, that we see what distinguishes us from all other living things and entitles us to think of ourselves as akin to the gods. Other creatures have no history and are virtually incapable of even the most trivial innovation or novelty. What was done by the generations that preceded them is done also by them in an endless repetition. But it is not so with human beings. Their works rise and fall, to be replaced by others that no one could have foreseen. Human beings, in a word, think, reflect, and *create*. It is no wonder that we are referred to in Scripture as having been created "in the image of God," for this has traditionally been thought of as the primary attribute of God, namely, that God is the *creator.*

Aristotle thought of the pursuit of knowledge as the human virtue par excellence. But it is significant that he thought of this, not merely as something passive, a mere absorption of things seen to be true, but rather as an activity. And it is the nature of intellectual activity that it is creative. To the extent that the mind is active, it is also creative, and this is true even in the sciences, and in such things as mathematics, where there is thought to be the least scope for novelty and innovation.

If we think of happiness as fulfillment, then it must consist of the fulfillment of ourselves as human beings, which means the exercise of our creative powers. For we are, among the creatures of the earth, the only ones possessed of such power. The idea of fulfillment is without meaning apart from the idea of function, however, and thus, as our bodies are fulfilled in health, so are our bodies and minds together fulfilled in creative activity. There are no real substitutes. The appearance of health, and the feelings associated with it, are often marks of that underlying state, but such things are not identical with it. The former can be present when the latter is not. And similarly, the appearance of happiness and the feeling of happiness are often marks of that precious state itself, but by no means to be confused with it. A person can appear happy and not be, and what is less readily understood, can feel happy and not be. Children, idiots, and animals, as we have seen, sometimes feel good, indeed, characteristically do; but they cannot possibly be happy in the true sense of the term. There simply is nothing more to be said of them with respect to their happiness than that they feel good.

Of course one might be tempted at this point to protest that if someone feels happy, what more can be wanted? Is it not quite enough to feel perfectly happy, without making much of the sources of that feeling? And why withhold the term *happiness* from anyone if that person is totally content with his own condition?

What more is wanted is, of course, the genuine thing. And one sees this readily enough if one imagines someone in whom the feelings of happiness are present, but the proper fulfillment of function is not, as again in the case of someone severely retarded. Whatever may be that person's feelings of self-satisfaction and joy, no one capable of a genuinely intelligent and creative life could ever trade it for this other. Feelings of joy complement and add to the happiness that most persons are capable of, but they can never replace it.

WHAT IS CREATIVITY?

When we think of creativity, we are apt to construe it narrowly, as the creation of things, sometimes even limiting it to things belonging to the arts. But this is arbitrary. Creative intelligence is exhibited by a dancer, by athletes, by a chess player, and indeed in virtually any activity guided by intelligence. In some respects the very paradigm of creative activity is the establishment of a brilliant position in a game of chess, even though what is created is of limited worth. Nor do such activities need to be the kind normally thought of as intellectual. For example, the exercise of skill in a profession, or in business, or even in such things as gardening and farming, or the rearing of a beautiful family, all such things are displays of creative intelligence. They can all be done badly or well and are always done *best* when done not by rule, rote, or imitation, but with successful originality. Nor is it hard to see that, in referring to such commonplace activities as these, at the same time we touch upon some of the greatest and most lasting sources of human happiness.

Consider, for example, something both commonplace and yet fairly unusual as begetting and rearing a beautiful family. There is, to be sure, nothing in the least creative about the mere begetting of children. It is something anyone can do. But to raise them and convert them to successful, that is, well-functioning, happy adults, requires great skill, intelligence, and creativity. We see this at once when we compare those who succeed at it with the many who do not. And now let us consider someone who has succeeded at this and ask what that person's happiness consists of, and how it compares with some of the specious substitutes for happiness that we have alluded to.

With respect to the first question, that is, what such a person's happiness consists of, we can easily see that it is not mere feeling. To be sure, the feelings of happiness are there, but they are based upon a state of being that is far more precious and enduring, namely, upon the lasting realization of what has been wrought. Feelings of reward, or of praise, or of envy in others, may be worth something; but if, for example, they rested upon nothing real, or upon actual error or misperception, then they would be worth very little. There would then be no real happiness behind them, but only the feelings of happiness. And with respect to the comparison of this person with someone whose happiness is perhaps spectacular but nonetheless specious, it is again not hard to see who is more blessed. Consider a man whose wealth far exceeds his needs and which has simply flowed to him without any creative effort on his part, as in the case of wealth that is inherited. This person cannot possibly have the happiness of even the most ordinary person who has created something valuable and lasting, even of a commonplace sort. To see this, you need only to get before your mind a clear image of both lives, and then ask not which one you envy, not which one is more honored by the masses of people, not which one shines with more glory, not which is filled with more feelings of exhilaration, but just simply: Which of these two persons is happier?

THE DEFEAT OF HAPPINESS

Happiness is often represented as something to be pursued, as something that might be conquered; and quite rightly, for this calls attention to the fact that it can also be lost, or that one might fail altogether to find it. It by no means flows automatically to those who wait for it, even when all the conditions for it are right. It must be chosen and sought.

Of course the clearest way in which it can be lost is by calamity, such as dreadful or life-destroying illness, and things of this nature, which either cannot be foreseen or cannot be warded off when they are foreseen. The Stoics maintained that even catastrophic setback or illness could not destroy one's happiness, but this was an extreme and unbelievable position. It is true that happiness cannot be conferred upon one, but it can certainly be taken away, and under some circumstances it is idle to speak of pursuing it.

The other ways in which one can fail to become happy are either: first, through ignorance of what happiness is, and hence an inability to distinguish genuine happiness from specious forms; or second, from lack of the creative intelligence necessary for its pursuit. We shall consider these in turn.

THE FAILURE FROM IGNORANCE

This has been dealt with incidentally. Thus, people who think happiness results from possession, for example, have no chance of becoming happy, for they go in the wrong direction. They may succeed in their pursuit of wealth, but having done that, they then find themselves using that wealth to pursue things equally specious, such as power over others or the envy of others, and other things totally unrelated to the kind of creative activity we have described; or else they find themselves going through the kinds of motions that have characterized their lives superfluously adding wealth to what they already have in great excess. The mere doing of things, perhaps on a large scale, achieves no more happiness than the mere defeat of boredom—for which, incidentally, most people appear quite willing to settle. Sheer boredom is indeed a baneful state. To escape it is, to some extent, a blessing though a negative one. Hence the incessant activity on the part of some—things done for no purpose beyond making more money; or travel undertaken for new sights and sounds passively absorbed; or projects pursued, sometimes on a grand scale, just to impress others; or things purchased for the same purpose. This is how many people live, escaping boredom, keeping busy, being preoccupied with something from one day to the next, giving little thought to life or to death. And this does achieve, for the moment, the banishment of boredom and loneliness; but that is as close to happiness as it gets. Meanwhile others who are wiser, having little of all this and almost never knowing boredom, go about life in their own way, creating from their own resources things original to themselves, quite unlike what others have done, things small, sometimes not small, sometimes even great and lasting, but every one of them something that is theirs and is the reflection of their own original power. Such people rejoice, perhaps unnoticed—and are happy.

THE WANT OF CREATIVE INTELLIGENCE

The second way to fail is through the sheer lack of what is needed to succeed. For if genuine happiness is found through the exercise of creative intelligence, then it is obvious that, without this, a person will have to be content with a specious kind of happiness, far less than the *eudaimonia* we have described. And many people, perhaps even most, are thus prevented.

Thus there are people whose every day is very much like the one just lived. They are essentially people without personal biographies except for the events which the mere passage of time thrusts upon them. In this they are like animals, each of whose lives is almost indistinguishable from others of its species, simply duplicating those of the generations before it. One sparrow does not differ from another. What it does, others have done and will do again, without creative improvement of any kind. Its life consists of what happens to it. And people who are like this have a similar uniformity. They do much as their neighbors do and as their parents have done, creating virtually no values of their own, but absorbing the values of those around them. Their lives are lived like clockwork, and thought, which should be the source of projects and ideals, is hardly more than a byproduct of what they are doing, an almost useless accompaniment like the ticking of a clock. You see these people everywhere, doing again today what they did yesterday, their ideas and feelings having about as little variation. And, it should be noted, such people are by the ordinary standards that prevail *quite happy*— that is, they are of good cheer, greet each sunrise with fresh anticipation, have friends, and spend much of their time exchanging empty remarks and pleasantries with others like them. They are, in a word, contented people who would declare with total sincerity, if asked, that they are perfectly happy, asking no more of the world than to escape those things, such as poverty or illness, which might threaten their contentment.

But we must not be misled by this. What such people have are certain feelings of happiness—feelings only. These are not bad, not even really illusory, but they do fall far short of the meaning of happiness the ancients tried to capture in the word *eudaimonia*. Such persons are not fulfilled but merely satisfied. They have a kind of contentment that is within the reach of anyone capable of suffering who luckily manages to escape suffering. What they have is not even distinctively personal or human. The measure of their happiness is nothing more than their lack of inclination to complain.

It is, to be sure, doubtful whether any normal person entirely fits this baneful description, but one can hardly fail to see that it expresses what is almost normal. Even the least creative among us are usually capable of something original, however innocuous it might be. But what is sad is that the kind of happiness that is within the reach only of human beings should be within the reach of so few of these. And what is sadder still is that those who have no clear idea of what happiness is, or worse, lack within themselves the resources to capture it, do not care. It is, in some ways, almost as if they had not even been born.

It is no wonder that the ancients thought of happiness as a blessing of almost divine worth, as something rare, and something that can be ascribed to someone only after he is dead.

Index

RICHARD TAYLOR
ETHICS, FAITH, AND REASON

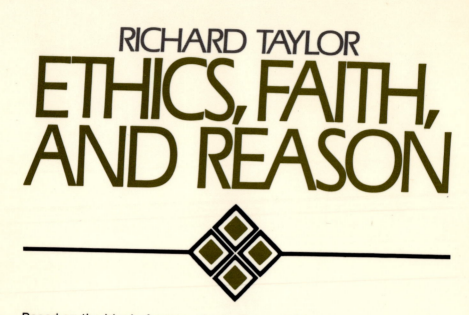

Based on the ideal of personal excellence, **Ethics, Faith, and Reason,** by Richard Taylor, is a radical departure from contemporary approaches to ethics.

In this new book, the author revives the ancient moral ideas of virtue, happiness, and pride rather than analyzing such concepts as moral right and wrong, moral obligation, and so on.

Among its features, the book:

- challenges the ethical framework inherited from the Judeo-Christian tradition
- offers a new appreciation of the ancient Greek moralists
- provides clearly-written, readily-grasped text
- develops material in such a way as to stimulate discussion

PRENTICE-HALL, INC., Englewood Cliffs, N.J. 07632

ISBN 0-13-290552-